Who's the Next President?

Who's the Next President?

KEN LAWLESS

Developed by
THE PHILIP LIEF GROUP, INC.

A Perigee Book

Perigee Books
are published by
The Putnam Publishing Group
200 Madison Avenue
New York, NY 10016

Photographs of Ivan Boesky, Michael Deaver, and Oliver North courtesy of
UPI/Bettmann Newsphotos. All other photographs courtesy of Celebrity Photos,
Los Angeles.

Library of Congress Cataloging-in-Publication Data

Lawless, Ken.
Who's the next president?

1. United States—Politics and government—
1981–   —Anecdotes, facetiae, satire, etc.
2. Presidents—United States—Election—1988—
Anecdotes, facetiae, satire, etc.   3. Political
satire, American.   I. Title.
E876.L39   1988   324.973'0927   87-7245
ISBN 0-399-51411-2

Typeset by Fisher Composition, Inc.

Printed in the United States of America
1   2   3   4   5   6   7   8   9   10

The Candidates

Kareem Abdul-Jabbar
Woody Allen
Howard Baker
Jim and Tammy Faye Bakker
Harry Belafonte
Ivan F. Boesky
William F. Buckley
Dale Bumpers
George Burns
George Bush
Al Capone
Amy Carter
Hernando Cortés
Bill Cosby
Tom Cruise
Mario Cuomo
Michael Deaver
Danny DeVito
Elizabeth Dole
Sam Donaldson
Michael Stanley Dukakis
Clint Eastwood
J. R. Ewing
Sarah Ferguson
Michael J. Fox
Whoopi Goldberg
Mr. Goodwrench
Raisa Maksimovna Gorbacheva

Albert Gore, Jr.
Spalding Gray
Fawn Hall
Warren Gamaliel Harding
Gary Hart
Max Headroom
Jesse Helms
Hulk Hogan
Sherlock Holmes
Dennis Hopper
Lee Iacocca
Jesse Jackson
Pope John Paul II
Jack Kemp
Adnan Khashoggi
Ed Koch
Dr. C. Everett Koop
Lyndon LaRouche, Jr.
Robin Leach
Huey Pierce Long
Ronald McDonald
Spuds MacKenzie
Shirley MacLaine
Ed McMahon
Madonna
Steve Martin
Groucho Marx
Edwin Meese III
John Stuart Mill
Mother Teresa
Eddie Murphy
Yasuhiro Nakasone
Jack Nicholson
Lieutenant Colonel Oliver North
Dolly Parton

Nancy Reagan
Ronald Reagan
Pat Robertson
Tom Selleck
William Shatner
Paul Simon
Bruce Springsteen
Sylvester Stallone
Howard Stern
Meryl Streep
Dr. Hunter S. Thompson
Lily Tomlin
Desmond Mpico Tutu
Peter Ueberroth
Dr. Ruth Westheimer
Vanna White
Bruce Willis
Oprah Winfrey
Ken Lawless

Kareem Abdul-Jabbar

EXPERIENCE: Mr. Abdul-Jabbar was copilot in the movie *Airplane.*

WINNABILITY: Mr. Abdul-Jabbar is the leading scorer in the history of the National Basketball Association, and six times its Most Valuable Player.

CAMPAIGN SLOGAN: "A President We Can All Look Up To"

PLATFORM: Mr. Abdul-Jabbar promises to hustle on defense.
Mr. Abdul-Jabbar promises to sit during public appearances such as press conferences and the State of the Union message so he won't make everybody else feel like a shrimp. (Hey, it worked in *Airport.* It even worked for FDR.)
Mr. Abdul-Jabbar promises mandatory drug tests for referees . . . during the game.
Mr. Abdul-Jabbar promises to use televised instant replays to investigate alleged Soviet violations of the SALT treaty.

RUNNING MATE: Emmanuel Lewis

SHADOW CABINET: Ambassador to Ireland: Larry Bird
Secretary of the Treasury: Tom Collins
Director of the CIA: Bill Walton
Surgeon General: Dr. Chap Stick (aka Dr. J)
Press Secretary: Lew Alcindor

PITFALL: Mr. Abdul-Jabbar, whose salary is $2 million per annum, is the sole stockholder and employee of the Delaware-based Ain Jeem Corporation, which is involved in complicated lawsuits over investments in hotels that went broke. Voters may worry that a guy who can't negotiate a real estate deal in California shouldn't be negotiating the future of the human race in Geneva.

Woody Allen

EXPERIENCE: Mr. Allen is a clarinet player who plays jazz every Monday night even if they happen to be giving him an Oscar someplace else. That's dedication. Or something.

WINNABILITY: Mr. Allen has created the persona of a nebbish for himself, somehow even managing to look the part. In spite of this, he has been romantically involved with some of the most glamorous women of the era—some of them shiksas yet! A nebbish who can score with gorgeous chicks can handle a little job, like CEO of only one branch of government.

CAMPAIGN SLOGAN: "Take the Money and Run"

PLATFORM: Mr. Allen promises that if he is elected President he will make funny movies instead of serious movies.
(That is Mr. Allen's only campaign promise, but it is the only pledge most of his fans want to hear anyway. It isn't even that they don't appreciate his serious movies, the ones that win the awards he can't be bothered accepting. . . . It's just that lots of folks can make serious movies, but if Woody Allen doesn't make Woody Allen movies, who will?

RUNNING MATE: Marshall Brickman

SHADOW CABINET: Secretary of Defense: Mel Brooks
Press Secretary: Tony Roberts
Attorney General: Louise Lasser

PITFALL: Mr. Allen is a bright New York liberal who began his career making jokes about Ike. Mr. Allen is versatile, energetic, and insightful enough to make a really good President—does George Bush or Bob Dole know more about human nature? can senators make a string of hit movies?—but the record suggests that bright New York liberals mustn't be too bright or too liberal, even in New York. After those Ike jokes, Mr. Allen might have trouble carrying Kansas.

Howard Baker

EXPERIENCE: Mr. Baker became a TV star during the Watergate hearings.

WINNABILITY: Because he became a TV star during the Watergate hearings, the moderate Republican senator from Tennessee has been running for President ever since, without ever convincing the fatcats to give him enough money to make him a contender. He is tenacious, though, which sometimes pays off for a Nixon and sometimes does not for a Stassen.

CAMPAIGN SLOGAN: "What Did the President Know and When Did the President Know It?"

PLATFORM: Mr. Baker promises to appoint Donald Regan to some posh diplomatic post to make up for Regan's hearing about Baker's replacing him as White House chief of staff on television.
Mr. Baker promises to have good relations with The Hill because as

a former senator he would be good at that—like former Senators Lyndon Johnson and Richard Nixon.

Mr. Baker promises to revitalize the economy by completing the Tennessee Tom project.

RUNNING MATE: Carroll Baker (aka Baby Doll)

SHADOW CABINET: Secretary of State: Edmund Muskie★
Secretary of Defense: John Tower★
National Security Adviser: Brent Scowcroft★

PITFALL: By taking the job as White House chief of staff, Mr. Baker left himself no time to run in '88. If the Democrats win in '88, Baker would face an incumbent in '92; if the Republicans win in '88, Baker would have to wait until *1996!* Rotten timing, Howie, rotten timing.

Jim and Tammy Faye Bakker

EXPERIENCE: This husband-and-wife team of successful entrepreneurs used to market cosmetics in a theme park and pie-in-the-sky on television. Mr. Bakker talked millions of people into mailing him hundreds of millions of dollars, so it is not surprising to learn that he may have talked to a few people into making whoopee.

WINNABILITY: If Jimmy Carter could be forgiven for lusting in his heart, perhaps the voters will forgive Jimmy Bakker for lusting in his loins.

CAMPAIGN SLOGAN: "Nine Out of Ten Ain't Bad"

★ As the Tower Commission, these three wrote the report that gave Nancy Reagan the ammo she needed to get rid of Don Regan to make way for her boy Howard Baker.

PLATFORM: The Bakkers promise if elected not to let themselves get quickly snookered out of power at the first whiff of scandal. If Reagan could smilingly stonewall his way through month after month of Iran-contra, Jim and Tammy ought to have been able to hang tough over a little hanky-panky.

RUNNING MATE: Ray Stevens

SHADOW CABINET: Secretary of Transportation: Aimee Semple McPherson
Secretary of the Treasury: Father Divine
Press Secretary: Reverend Ike
Ambassador to Guyana: Jim Jones
Ambassador to Hell: Charles Shepard

PITFALL: American charismatic religious leaders are often accused of hanky-panky. A partial list would include some early Mormon leaders, John Humphrey Noyes of the Perfectionists, Elijah Pierson and the Matthias Cult, and Benjamin Purnell of the House of David. Americans who pretend to be shocked by the interplay of sex and religion have been reading neither their history books nor their Bibles. Voters willing to forgive Mr. Bakker for Jessica Hahn may balk at reports suggesting that host is both PTL and AC/DC.

Harry Belafonte

EXPERIENCE: Mr. Belafonte used to sing with his shirtfront open even in the 1950s when most men had their shirts, their cuffs, their collars, and their brains buttoned down. Back then, reggae was called calypso and Mr. Belafonte was its harbinger.

WINNABILITY: Lots of people think that Mr. Belafonte's Godfather in *Uptown Saturday Night* was better than Brando's Godfather in *The Godfather.* (Brando's may have been funnier, but Belafonte's

had more menace.) A guy who can out-Brando Brando, sing like Bob Marley, talk like Ronald Colman, and look like a matinee idol has got to have winnability. (And his daughters are more famous than Tricia Nixon, Maureen Reagan, or Amy Carter.)

CAMPAIGN SLOGAN: "Day-o! Day-ay-ay-o! Belafonte Will Go All the Way-ay-ay-o!"

PLATFORM: Mr. Belafonte promises to remake *Carmen Jones*, doing his own singing.

RUNNING MATE: Sidney Poitier

SHADOW CABINET: Secretary of Education: Floyd Patterson *

PITFALL: Mr. Belafonte has probably done more discreet work for charities and worthy causes than any star of his magnitude. A suc-

---

*Mr. Patterson has done fine work with young people and raised money for his alma mater, the Wiltwyck School for Boys. He would make a better secretary of education than . . . guess whom? If you thought I was kidding, the joke is on you. We need some imaginative appointments to cabinet posts.

cessful producer and entrepreneur, Mr. Belafonte seems to have the ability and the character to make a wonderful President. To judge from the record, Americans don't nominate or elect people like that. Not lately.

Ivan F. Boesky

EXPERIENCE: Mr. Boesky is a student of the American system of high finance.

WINNABILITY: When the Securities and Exchange Commission caught Mr. Boesky violating guidelines that prohibit the abuse of inside information in the buying and selling of stocks, it penalized him with the highest fine it had ever levied. Americans love superlatives.

CAMPAIGN SLOGAN: "When Ivan Boesky Talks, E. F. Hutton Listens"

PLATFORM: Mr. Boesky promises to use inside tips to reduce the trade deficit.

RUNNING MATE: Robert Vesco

SHADOW CABINET:
Press Secretary: Louis Rukeyser
Secretary of the Treasury:
Willy "The Lion" Sutton
National Security Council:
The IMF (No, not the
International Monetary
Fund: the Impossible
Mission Force!)

PITFALL: Despite his impressive qualifications, the American people may not be ready for a President named Ivan. "President Ivan" sounds too much like a bad joke from *Amerika* or *Red Dawn*.

William F. Buckley

EXPERIENCE: Mr. Buckley is a TV talk-show host with more experience albeit less soul than Oprah Winfrey.

WINNABILITY: Mr. Buckley is considered by many liberals to be the most winsome reactionary in the land, giving him a potentially broader base of support than most right-wing ideologues.

CAMPAIGN SLOGAN: "Let Buckley Be Buckley"

PLATFORM: Mr. Buckley promises not to use any big words unless George Will can define them without a dictionary.
Mr. Buckley promises to remain simple and unaffected even in the Oval Office, combining as always the snide with the Lincolnesque.
Mr. Buckley promises to be reasonable with commies from Russia in return for preventive detention for domestic com-symp/lib-lab/parlor-pinko/peace-creeps who have always been his real enemies.
Mr. Buckley promises not to write any more of those awful spy thrillers.

RUNNING MATE: Jeane Kirkpatrick

SHADOW CABINET: Secretary of State: James Buckley
Secretary of Defense: Norman Mailer*
Secretary of Education: Gore Vidal*

PITFALL: Voters may be reluctant to deprive PBS of its longtime pet reactionary.

*Ostensibly antagonists of Mr. Buckley, these individuals are actually fellow clowns in the media circus, hitting one another with pig bladders.

Dale Bumpers

EXPERIENCE: Mr. Bumpers is a senator from Arkansas. He is known as a "giant-killer" for consistently defeating much more famous opponents, including Orval Faubus, Winthrop Rockefeller, and J. William Fulbright.

WINNABILITY: Giant-killer he would have to be because few candidates are less famous than Dale Bumpers. Most voters probably think "dale bumpers" is a game played at fraternity parties. The affable, low-key senator wanted to ration gasoline in 1977. That may have been the prudent, enlightened policy but Americans do *not* want their gasoline rationed. They would rather bomb those towel-headed camel jockeys into their sand dunes than wait in line at the pump with a ration card.

CAMPAIGN SLOGAN: "This Dale Is Not Mondale"

PLATFORM: Mr. Bumpers promises not to smoke, drink, or cuss . . . in public.
Mr. Bumpers promises that he plays the trumpet as well as Harry Truman played the piano.

RUNNING MATE: Dale Robertson

SHADOW CABINET: Secretary of Transportation: Dale Evans
Speechwriters: Smith and Dale
National Security Council: The Jimmy Dale Orchestra
Press Secretary: Aldo Sigismundi*

PITFALL: Even his ardent supporters might feel silly sticking Bumpers bumper stickers on their bumpers.

---

*Aka Alan Dale.

George Burns

EXPERIENCE: George Burns has already been God, not once but twice, and many voters seem to feel that the President is or ought to be an anthropomorphic deity. Besides, having served two terms as God, Mr. Burns is ready to try the more difficult job.

WINNABILITY: Mr. Burns is the most likable man on the planet and could win free elections in Poland, China, or El Salvador if those places knew there was such a thing as free elections.

CAMPAIGN SLOGAN: "Good Night, Gracie!"

PLATFORM: Mr. Burns promises to sing at his inaugural ball. Mr. Burns promises to croon a tune at any summit conferences.

RUNNING MATE: John Denver

SHADOW CABINET: Secretary of Education: Gracie Allen
Secretary of State: Fred Allen
Secretary of the Interior: Steve Allen
Secretary of Commerce: Woody Allen
Secretary of the Treasury: Jack Benny
Surgeon General: Groucho Marx

PITFALL: Only one thing threatens the landslide victory of George Burns: some voters may be confused by the similarity of his name with that of George Bush, and George Bush is *not* funny.

George Bush

EXPERIENCE: Mr. Bush was head of the CIA. As Vice President, he seems to have thought he was empowered to run his own private little CIA.

WINNABILITY: Mr. Bush is the frontrunner for the 1988 Republican nomination as this reference book goes to press. He has certainly paid his dues to the party regulars who run the machinery.

His ability to beat Bob Dole in a primary is a *big* question mark. As both a northeastern preppie and a Texan, his image covers the Republican spectrum. Besides, he was right to call Reagan's ideas "Voodoo Economics" in 1980.

CAMPAIGN SLOGAN: "Push for Bush"

PLATFORM: Mr. Bush promises to identify himself with Ronald Reagan while he distances himself from Ronald Reagan. Mr. Bush promises to exorcise the Voodoo Economics he has supported for eight years.

RUNNING MATE: Jim Baker*

SHADOW CABINET: Attorney General: Lee Atwater**
Speechwriter: Landon Parvin
Guardian Angel: William Casey (if he isn't too busy haunting Bob Woodward)

PITFALL: Having lost the nomination to Ronald Reagan in 1980 by seeming too moderate, Mr. Bush has spent eight years wooing the Republican Right with some success only to find himself tarnished by the Iran/Contragate misadventures. He may lose to Bob Dole, erstwhile right-wing hatchet man who moderated his image and moved toward the center.

Al Capone

EXPERIENCE: Mr. Capone is a successful entrepreneur whose career has been glamorized in a number of films.

*That's Jim Baker with one *k*, the guy who swapped jobs with Don Regan with one *a*, not Jim Bakker with two *k*s who is accused of sexual and fiscal hanky-panky while heading the PTL Club.

**This would perpetuate the appalling new tradition of rewarding the successful campaign manager by giving him the Department of Justice to manipulate.

WINNABILITY: Mr. Capone's initiatives were thwarted by the Internal Revenue Service. Most Americans hate the IRS, and this gives Mr. Capone a reservoir of sympathy.

CAMPAIGN SLOGAN: "A Vote for Me Is an Offer You Can't Refuse"

PLATFORM: Mr. Capone promises to give the Ayatollah cement slippers for his swimming lessons.
President Capone promises to restore Havana to its rightful owners, the Mob.

RUNNING MATE: Carlo Gambino

SHADOW CABINET*: Secretary of State: Dutch Schultz
Secretary of the Interior: Machine-Gun Kelly
Secretary of the Treasury: Arnold Rothstein
Press Secretary: Baby-Face Nelson
Secretary of Transportation: The Lady in Red

PITFALL: Mr. Capone may have embarrassed Geraldo Rivera when his supposed treasure vault turned up empty. This could cost him media support.

Amy Carter

EXPERIENCE: Ms. Carter advised a former President about nuclear disarmament prior to a key debate.

WINNABILITY: Americans seem addicted to political dynasties, touting the offspring of any Kennedy or Nixon as potential leaders. Amy could help satisfy the American lust for hereditary rulers.

*Note the ethnic balance. Mr. Capone's industry has long practiced equal opportunity.

CAMPAIGN SLOGAN: "Amy Is No Wimp"

PLATFORM: Ms. Amy promises to catheterize her Uncle Billy.
Ms. Amy promises patient diplomacy regarding hostages, noting that her father got Americans back from Iran without swapping enough arms to kill thousands of Iraqis . . . or thousands of anybody the Ayatollah doesn't like.
Ms. Amy promises to put more pressure on South Africa than "constructive engagement" and to oppose illegal shenanigans by the CIA even if she risks limited probation at Brown.

RUNNING MATE: John-John Kennedy

SHADOW CABINET: Secretary of the Navy: Jimmy Carter
Press Secretary: Michael Reagan*
Ambassador to China: Tricia Nixon Eisenhower
Éminence grise: Abbie Hoffman

PITFALL: After the elegance and glamour of Nancy Reagan's White House, the electorate may be reluctant to return to the tacky, down-home ambience of a Carter administration. Why, President Amy might try to carry her own luggage or something outrageous like that!

Hernando Cortés

EXPERIENCE: Mr. Cortés was the conquistador who had to defeat the Aztec empire while also fighting his own faction—this is the perfect experience for a Democratic candidate.

---

*When the space shuttle *Challenger* exploded on launch a few hours before President Reagan's State of the Union address was scheduled to begin, Michael told a Los Angeles TV audience, "That'll be a tough act for Dad to follow." A press secretary who says what he thinks might be a refreshing change.

WINNABILITY: A guy who can defeat an empire with a handful of mutinous troops ought to be able to handle the likes of Michael Dukakis and Bob Dole.

CAMPAIGN SLOGAN: "I Burned My Boats (and If You Get Out of Line, I'll Burn Your Boats Too)"

PLATFORM: Mr. Cortés promises to do to Qaddafi what he did to Montezuma.
Mr. Cortés promises to do to the Ayatollah what he did to Montezuma.
Mr. Cortés promises to pay Mexico's foreign debt if Mexico promises no more American *turistas* will suffer Montezuma's revenge.

RUNNING MATE: Francisco Pizarro

SHADOW CABINET: Secretary of Defense: Lope de Aguirre, the Wrath of God
Secretary of State: Antonio López de Santa Anna
Ambassador to the United Nations: Pancho Villa
Press Secretary: Sancho Panza

PITFALL: If the United States wants an empire in Central America, it ought to send the best, but if the voters reflect on the sorry history of empires they may decide that *primus inter pares* is a better idea for this hemisphere than *imperium in imperio*, making election night another *noche triste* for Mr. Cortés.

Bill Cosby

EXPERIENCE: Mr. Cosby was the predecessor of Max Headroom as the corporate spokesperson for Coca-Cola. He is the successor to Ozzie Nelson and Robert Young as TV's perfect Dad.

WINNABILITY: A guy who symbolizes Coca-Cola and family values could garner a lot of votes. A guy who can shill for gelatinous desserts *and* stockbrokers has really broad appeal. Throw in his being smart and funny and you could have a winner at the polls.

CAMPAIGN SLOGAN: "It's *My* Money"

PLATFORM: Mr. Cosby promises to write his own material for the State of the Union address.
Mr. Cosby promises that his experience in espionage will enable him to put the kibosh on all these spy scandals.

RUNNING MATE: Earvin Johnson★

SHADOW CABINET: Fat Albert and the Cosby Kids will rotate among cabinet posts.
Robert Culp will become ambassador to Moscow.

PITFALL: White voters may suspect the presence of a hidden volcano of suppressed anger beneath that genial surface. Virtually all whites suspect virtually all blacks of suppressing hidden rage while virtually all blacks suspect virtually all whites of suppressing hidden vestiges of racism. Mr. Cosby's high ratings may not be translatable into votes, after all.

★Even the Cosby candidacy would benefit from some "Magic." If Mr. Cosby is at all superstitious, he may not want to risk a Vice President named Johnson: the last two guys who tried it got shot.

Tom Cruise

EXPERIENCE: Mr. Cruise is top gun in a risky business who knows the color of money.

WINNABILITY: Mr. Cruise is probably the most wholesome member of Hollywood's Brat Pack. He is so polite that Martin Scorsese had a hard time getting Mr. Cruise to stop calling him "Sir." This guy is so all-American that even his name is the same as our most effective missile.

CAMPAIGN SLOGAN: "Cruise with Cruise"

PLATFORM: As Hollywood insider and star of *The Outsiders*, Mr. Cruise promises to be President of all the people.
Mr. Cruise promises that the Ramboesque commie-bashing of *Top Gun* was only entertainment, like *Red Dawn* and *Amerika*.

RUNNING MATE: Emilio Estevez

SHADOW CABINET: Cabinet officers will include Brat Packers Matt Dillon, Rob Lowe, and Timothy Hutton. Sean Penn is committed to Madonna's candidacy.

PITFALL: Older voters who have been gaga about Paul Newman since they first saw his knees in 1954's *The Silver Chalice* may find it difficult to forgive Mr. Cruise for supplanting his Fast Eddie.

Mario Cuomo

EXPERIENCE: To become two-term governor of New York, Mr. Cuomo defeated such formidable Republican opponents as . . . uh . . . as . . . er, does anybody remember either of those names?

WINNABILITY: Mr. Cuomo made a good speech at the 1984 Democratic Convention. The Democratic Party is in such sad shape that even one good speech makes for a leading contender. Mr. Cuomo has been taken to task by pundits for saying he does not want to run for President, but the average voter has a grudging admiration for the good sense of anyone unwilling to play the fool for the media sideshow we call a campaign.

CAMPAIGN SLOGAN: "If Nominated, I Will Not Run; If Elected, Well, Maybe"

PLATFORM: Mr. Cuomo promises to sponsor a constitutional amendment making it a federal crime to joke about Italians and the Mafia.

RUNNING MATE: General Sherman

SHADOW CABINET: Attorney General: Andrew Cuomo
Press Secretary: Al Capone
National Security Council: The Mafia (Hey, Mario, we're only *kidding*, for crying out loud!)

PITFALL: Mr. Cuomo started a poisonous feud with the working press just after a landslide election victory had everyone touting him as a likely President in 1988. If he is that thin-skinned when he is winning, the voters may have doubts about his ability to stay cool in the pressure cooker we call the Oval Office.

Michael Deaver

EXPERIENCE: Mr. Deaver was deputy chief of staff in the Reagan White House.

WINNABILITY: Mr. Deaver has been indicted for abuse of the public trust. It might be a relief for the voters to have a President begin his administration that way instead of having to cope with the problem down the line.

CAMPAIGN SLOGAN:
"Leave It to Deaver"

PLATFORM: Mr. Deaver promises to get as rich as possible while in the Oval Office. Mr. Deaver promises to become a brain surgeon after serving as President.
Mr. Deaver promises to help TWA and Canada no matter how long it takes.

RUNNING MATE: Jerry Mathers*

SHADOW CABINET: Secretary of the Treasury: Bert Lance
Secretary of the Interior: Spiro Agnew
Secretary of the Air Force: D. B. Cooper
National Security Adviser: Ferdinand Marcos
Press Secretary: G. Gordon Liddy

PITFALL: If Mr. Deaver is in prison during the campaign, the stripes on his prison garb may make a poor impression during the all-important televised debates.

*That gives us the Dream Ticket of Michael Deaver/Beaver Cleaver.

Danny DeVito

EXPERIENCE: Mr. DeVito was an energetic albeit hyperactive dispatcher for the Sunshine Cab Company in New York City, where a cabbie is a cabbie is a cabbie.

WINNABILITY: Mr. DeVito is hot, and as everyone knows, when you are hot you are hot.

CAMPAIGN SLOGAN: "I Can Make America Stand Tall"

PLATFORM: Shoes. Mr. DeVito promises that his White House team will be tin men willing to throw mama from the train for the sake of the country.

RUNNING MATE: Randy Newman

SHADOW CABINET: Press Secretary: Richard Dreyfuss
Secretary of Education: Judd Hirsch
Éminence grise: Mickey Rooney
First Lady: Rhea Perlman
National Security Council: Ruthless People

PITFALL: Americans have made some small but heartening progress in overcoming bigotry based on racial or ethnic factors, but we remain prejudiced against short people. We admire "a man you can look up to" and disdain "a man you can look down on." The only women who will date men shorter than they are in high heels are mobsters' molls. We admire Abraham Lincoln in part because he was "Lincolnesque," meaning long-shanked, and we dismiss Martin Van Buren as small fry.

Enlightened as we hope we are, we Americans may not yet be ready to accept a short President. The opposition party would have a field day with old chestnuts like: "Did you hear why the President was banned from the nudist colony? He kept putting his nose in everybody else's business."

Elizabeth Dole

EXPERIENCE: Mrs. Dole was Secretary of Transportation in the Reagan cabinet until she resigned to devote herself to her husband's campaign for the Presidency.

WINNABILITY: Mrs. Dole is considered the strongest woman candidate in the United States. This is the political equivalent of damnation-by-faint-praise. Male pundits use the defeat of Geraldine Ferraro as proof that the nation is not ready for a female Vice President, ignoring the fact that Walter Mondale was such a weak candidate that he would have lost with George Washington as a running mate.

CAMPAIGN SLOGAN: "Behind Every Ambitious Man Is a Talented Woman Sacrificing her Career for His"

PLATFORM: Mrs. Dole promises executive clemency for Michael Deaver, who got in dutch for lobbying her department on behalf of TWA.
Mrs. Dole promises not to let her spouse run the nation, a mistake Nancy Reagan is said to have made before she dumped Don Regan and assumed direct control of the government.

RUNNING MATE: Jimmy Hoffa★

SHADOW CABINET: Secretary of Transportation: Robert Dole

★Mr. Hoffa is in seclusion, not having been seen in public recently, but he should emerge from his isolation for the honor of running for the Vice Presidency. He is an expert on Transportation, though he may not have remembered to arrange for a getaway car.

Women's rights activists are extremely irked by Mrs. Dole's decision to abandon her own career for the trite ceremonial role as candidate's spouse. Now, if only *Bob* Dole had quit *his* government job to work for *her* campaign, she could have beaten the likes of George Bush and the Seven Democratic Dwarfs by a landslide.

Sam Donaldson

EXPERIENCE: Mr. Donaldson is ABC White House correspondent, to the usual chagrin of White House incumbents.

WINNABILITY: Mr. Donaldson has the all-American good looks now considered essential in a Presidential candidate (no Lincolns need apply); he is a skilled performer on the key medium of television. He would probably also qualify as the first Presidential author since Woodrow Wilson whose books were not ghosted for him.

CAMPAIGN SLOGAN: "Now There I Go Again"

PLATFORM: Mr. Donaldson promises to be as candid during his press conferences as the Presidents he grilled were not.
Mr. Donaldson promises to reveal the identity of Deep Throat.

RUNNING MATE: John Peter Zenger

SHADOW CABINET:
Press Secretary: Dustin Hoffman or Robert Redford
State Department Spokesperson: Robert Redford or Dustin Hoffman
(Mr. Donaldson will appoint Redford and Hoffman instead of the real Woodward and Bernstein because the nation can spare two good actors more than it can three good journalists. Besides, after *Ishtar* Mr. Hoffman may need the job.)

PITFALL: Mr. Donaldson told Johnny Carson that he thinks President Reagan would give a poor person the clothes off his back, he is that generous, but then sit down in his underwear and sign legislation depriving millions of poor people of benefits. Talking about a President in his underwear is an instance of the sin of lèse majesté which many Americans will never forgive Mr. Donaldson for.

Michael Stanley Dukakis

EXPERIENCE: Mr. Dukakis has been governor of Massachusetts since 1975. Senator Biden said governors lack experience in foreign policy but Massachusetts is so liberal it voted for *McGovern* for President in 1972 and its relations with ultraconservative states are a lot like foreign policy. (P.S. Mr. Dukakis sure got even with Senator Biden for that little gibe.)

WINNABILITY: With his balanced budget and his workfare, Mr. Dukakis is largely indistinguishable from moderate Republicans in the Northeast, who are apt to support Mr. Dukakis against a right-wing Republican.

CAMPAIGN SLOGAN: "Dukakis Is One of *Your* Advocates"

PLATFORM: Mr. Dukakis promises a no-fault foreign policy. Mr. Dukakis promises to provide all his opponents with *The Compleat Speeches of Neil Kinnock.*

RUNNING MATE: Anyone or Anything named Kennedy

SHADOW CABINET: White House Chief of Staff: Arthur Beaulieu* CIA Director: John Sasso

PITFALL: As a first-generation Greek-American, Mr. Dukakis may have trouble carrying the Turkish vote.

Clint Eastwood

EXPERIENCE: Mr. Eastwood began as a high-plains drifter who worked for a fistful of dollars. He is now a wealthy man. America likes self-made millionaires.

---

* *The New York Times* reported in 1978 that Boston Police Sergeant Arthur Beaulieu, assigned to the governor, had such strikingly similar handwriting that he signed routine documents for Mr. Dukakis. Since signing documents is what a President does, Mr. Beaulieu would be a handy fella to have around.

WINNABILITY: Mr. Eastwood is an elected official from California who costarred with a chimpanzee in a popular movie. Does that sound familiar? It is the perfect formula for winnability.

CAMPAIGN SLOGAN: "Go Ahead, Ayatollah . . . Make My Day!"

PLATFORM: Mr. Eastwood promises *not* to let the Bill of Rights irk the cop on the beat.
Mr. Eastwood promises to keep the sun at his back.
Mr. Eastwood promises to be a President of *all* the people—the good, the bad, and the ugly.

RUNNING MATE: Clyde

SHADOW CABINET:
Press Secretary:
Norman Mailer
Secretary of Defense:
Chuck Norris
National Security Council:
The Dirty Dozen

PITFALL: When the electorate realizes that a nuclear war would litter the streets of San Francisco with even more dead bodies than Dirty Harry Callahan did, they may turn Mr. Eastwood every which way but loose.

J. R. Ewing

EXPERIENCE: Mr. Ewing is the ruthlessly unscrupulous oil tycoon from *Dallas*.

WINNABILITY: As the man Americans love to hate, Mr. Ewing could draw as many votes as Richard Nixon, whose 1972 victory was one of the largest landslides ever. Besides, Mr. Ewing was once a cheerful astronaut with his own genie and later enjoyed *The Good Life* with Donna Mills. Americans expect their President to be a charming, ordinary guy most of the time but occasionally tougher than Attila the Hun. J.R. has the track record.

CAMPAIGN SLOGAN: "Vita Celebratio Est" ★

PLATFORM: Mr. Ewing promises never to appear in public without his hat. Mr. Ewing promises that he has the most experience in dealing with Washington's number-one problem: corruption.

RUNNING MATE: Victoria Principal

SHADOW CABINET: Shuttle Diplomat: Patrick Duffy
Press Secretary: Mary Martin

PITFALL: Mr. Ewing in one of his avatars has been active against smoking. This could cost him a lot of votes, especially in North Carolina, where a guy who packs a battery-operated fan to blow smoke back at smokers might find himself less popular in a place called Winston-Salem than any crooked businessman could ever be in big-*D* little-*a* double-*l a-s*.

★ "Life is a party."

Sarah Ferguson

EXPERIENCE: Ms. Ferguson married one of those Hanoverian princes. Let's see . . . it wasn't Charles, he's half of Chuck and Lady Di. It wasn't Edward, he's the draft-dodger who didn't want to be a Royal Marine. Fergie latched onto Andrew, the one who went to the Falklands and messed around with Koo Stark. A real *prince,* anyway.

WINNABILITY: Fergie is so amiable she has dethroned Lady Di as the darling of the tabloids, even if her antics do occasionally raise a royal eyebrow on her mother-in-law. The way millions of Americans dote on the doings of descendants of George III makes it better-than-even money that Fergie could beat a George Bush or a Paul Simon.

CAMPAIGN SLOGAN: "I Am *Not* Pudgy!"

PLATFORM: Ms. Ferguson promises to visit any crazy royals discovered by the press in remote asylums.
Ms. Ferguson promises to open the archives in Windsor Castle so Yanks can find out whether Jack the Ripper was a royal.

RUNNING MATE: Princess Caroline

SHADOW CABINET: Secretary of State: Tina Turner★
Attorney General: Craig Russell★★

PITFALL: Gossip about the British royal family is less reliable than the year-end predictions of psychics or the economic forecasts of the Federal Reserve Board, so it is impossible to believe a word you read about Fergie. Why, she might be an ordinary nice person! *That* would disqualify her for the Presidency. The last ordinary nice person we had in the White House was McKinley, who campaigned from his front porch in Ohio, and we all remember what happened to *him.*

★Tina Turner is the Queen of Rock and Roll, a richer realm than Blimey.

★★Craig Russell is the world's best Drag Queen.

Michael J. Fox

EXPERIENCE: Mr. Fox is the hottest personality in American show biz. This is perhaps a left-handed compliment since his chief rivals are a computer-generated Brit and a letter-turning bimbo, but he is still *very* hot.

WINNABILITY: Mr. Fox offers a violent society a completely non-threatening image. He looks like the perfect first date for Everyman's daughter. Shorter than Dustin Hoffman, cuter than Tom Brokaw, more fastidious than Mr. Belvedere, he is the preppiest preppie of them all.

CAMPAIGN SLOGAN:
"Family Ties Are the Secret of My Success"

PLATFORM: Mr. Fox promises not to play hockey in the White House.*
Mr. Fox promises to give up his $70,000 Ferrari for a mere Presidential limo.
Mr. Fox promises to take the whole nation back to the future.

RUNNING MATE: Alex Keaton

SHADOW CABINET: Secretary of the Treasury: Brantley Foster

PITFALL: The name Fox is not Presidential. Some wags might be tempted to use vulgar puns. Besides, the last time we had a Fox in the White House (Martin Van Buren, the Sly Red Fox of Kinderhook), the nation suffered from a terrible economic depression.

---

*Mr. Fox got fifty-six stitches in his face for an injury from playing hockey in his native Canada, where that sort of thing is common as snowflakes. Fox is, like Donald Sutherland and Rich Little, further proof that Canadians make the best Americans.

Whoopi Goldberg

EXPERIENCE: Ms. Goldberg was hairdresser in a mortuary, a calling she shares with another irrepressible comedienne, the delightful Miss Mowcher in *David Copperfield*. Perhaps this calling is an inducement to mirth.

WINNABILITY: Ms. Goldberg is more likable than a spaniel puppy. She is also a born mimic who could pretend to be Lincolnesque or Ike-esque or whatever-esque the pollsters said the voters were hankering to have. With a name like Goldberg, she ought to carry the Jewish vote.

CAMPAIGN SLOGAN:
"Let's Make Whoopi . . .
the Next President"

PLATFORM: Ms. Goldberg, whose career was launched with her one-woman "Spook Show," promises that not even CIA spooks will be in her administration. Ms. Goldberg promises to keep her real name a secret, just like a superhero—the Lone Ranger, Batman, Superman, et al.

RUNNING MATE: Soupy Sales

SHADOW CABINET: Campaign Manager: Mike Nichols
Attorney General: Mike Nichols

PITFALL: Her original pseudonym was Whoopi Cushion (with a very French pronunciation). Voters who gave Gary Hart a bad time for changing his name may have qualms about a President who used to be named Whoopi Cushion.

Mr. Goodwrench

EXPERIENCE: Mr. Goodwrench is a versatile individual who is both automobile mechanic and corporate symbol.

WINNABILITY: Although he works repairing automobiles, Mr. Goodwrench always has hands and shirts as clean as a brain surgeon. He often fixes cars *without charge!* Since Americans like their kids but adore their cars, he should garner votes.

CAMPAIGN SLOGAN: "I Will Balance America's Wheels and America's Budget in Five Years or 50 Billion Miles"

PLATFORM: Mr. Goodwrench will install airbags in the F-15. Mr. Goodwrench will put the economy into overdrive.

RUNNING MATE: Mr. Clean

SHADOW CABINET: Secretary of the Interior: Mr. Whipple
Chief of Protocol: Mr. Goodbar
Secretary of the Navy: Mr. Roberts
Secretary of the Treasury: Mr. 880
Ambassador to France: Mr. Hulot
CIA Director: Mr. Moto
Secretary of Agriculture: Mr. Majestyk
Press Secretary: Mr. Completely

PITFALL: Mr. Goodwrench is owned by a major corporation, but this is hardly a first for American politicians. If you asked most Americans which they would rather have, an honest President or an honest automobile mechanic, most would burst into spontaneous laughter at so preposterous a question. Mr. Goodwrench may lack credibility.

Raisa Maksimovna Gorbacheva

EXPERIENCE: Mrs. Gorbachev is First Lady of the Union of Soviet Socialist Republics.

WINNABILITY: The KGB got pictures of Mrs. Gorbachev on a shopping spree in London with her American Express Gold Card. This ought to endear her to the American business community and to American consumers.

CAMPAIGN SLOGAN: "Shopski Till You Dropski"

PLATFORM: Mrs. Gorbachev promises to get her husband a wig from Carl Reiner.
Mrs. Gorbachev promises that because of *glasnost* she will not send the cast of *Amerika* to the gulag.

RUNNING MATE: Mikhail Whatchamacallnik

SHADOW CABINET: Mrs. Gorbachev will form an American politburo by combining the Tri-Lateral Commission with the National Association of Manufacturers and the AFL-CIO. (Not what you would expect? Hey, she has a big country to run and she can't do that with outsiders like American Socialist Party leader Michael Harrington.)

PITFALL: Imelda Marcos may have tarnished the image of wives of heads-of-state who go on shopping sprees.

Albert Gore, Jr.

EXPERIENCE: Mr. Gore is, like his father Albert Sr. before him, a Democratic senator from Tennessee. He was among the first to announce his candidacy in 1987 and at thirty-nine is the youngest.

WINNABILITY: Mr. Gore would stand an excellent chance of carrying Knoxville, Nashville, Chattanooga, Jackson, Memphis, and, indeed, the entire state of Tennessee.

CAMPAIGN SLOGAN: "Youth Refreshes"

PLATFORM: Mr. Gore promises he is for competitiveness and excellence, against the arms race and AIDS. *That* should distinguish him from other candidates.

RUNNING MATE: Tennessee Ernie Ford

SHADOW CABINET: Secretary of State: Van Heflin*
Secretary of the Interior: John Payne**
Press Secretary: a Tennessee Walking Horse descended from Mr. Ed.

PITFALL: As an unknown southern Democrat, Mr. Gore may remind people of Jimmy Carter in 1976. Reminding people of Jimmy Carter is a no-no in Presidential politics.

Spalding Gray

EXPERIENCE: Mr. Gray helped in the making of the movie *The Killing Fields*. He believes it would be easier to swim to Cambodia than to grasp the magnitude of the tragedy there.

*Mr. Heflin played the title role in *Tennessee Johnson*.
**Mr. Payne was Tennessee in *Tennessee's Partner*. Guess who played the partner?

WINNABILITY: Mr. Gray has the gift of gab. Most speakers become boring within minutes but Mr. Gray is still captivating after an hour and a half. One pundit called his political ideas "cosmic twaddle" but voters may find that no worse than business-as-usual. Mr. Gray proves that the energy level of talking about ordinary life is higher than the energy level of living it. He could get a lot of votes by giving voice to the Thoreauvian masses leading their lives of quiet desperation.

CAMPAIGN SLOGAN: "Talk Is Cheap"

PLATFORM: Mr. Gray promises to work from a polymorphous perverse state.
Mr. Gray will talk the ears off the Russians in negotiations until they accept our terms in sheer desperation.

RUNNING MATE: Andre Gregory★

SHADOW CABINET: Ambassador to Denmark: Hamlet

PITFALL: Americans will not appreciate being reminded, however obliquely, that it was our secret and illegal bombing of Cambodia that acted as catalyst in the tragedy. Most Americans want to get their images of Vietnam from *Magnum, P.I.*, not from some brilliant blabbermouth and city slicker like Spalding Gray.

Fawn Hall

EXPERIENCE: Ms. Hall is skilled in the use of office equipment, e.g., the shredder.

★ The loquacious star of *My Dinner with Andre* may be the only person in America who could get a word in edgewise while sharing the ticket with Mr. Gray.

WINNABILITY: Ms. Hall is more photogenic than the other candidates from the political milieu. Since television will determine the ultimate winner, this is a significant asset.

CAMPAIGN SLOGAN: "Vote for a Candidate Who Already Has Immunity"

PLATFORM: Ms. Hall promises to rewrite any documents that might embarrass her administration.
Ms. Hall pledges herself to win the swimsuit competition against Mrs. Gorbachev, Margaret Thatcher, and Corazon Aquino.
Ms. Hall promises not to help her old boss Ollie North funnel millions of dollars to her old contra boyfriend, Arturo Cruz, Jr.

RUNNING MATE: Rita Jenrette

SHADOW CABINET: Secretary of the Treasury: Monty Hall
Ambassador to the United Nations: Annie Hall
Secretary of Commerce: Huntz Hall
Secretary of the Interior: Faneuil Hall
Ambassador to the Court of St. James: Albert Hall
National Security Council: Hall and Oates

PITFALL: Farrah Fawcett was reported in *Time* as planning to portray Ms. Hall in a film biography. A thing like that could sink the candidacy of George Washington.

Warren Gamaliel Harding

EXPERIENCE: Mr. Harding was President from 1921 until his death on August 2, 1923. Despite his brief tenure of office, a 1962 poll of historians ranked Mr. Harding as the very *worst* President.

WINNABILITY: Mr. Harding looks a lot better by comparison now than he did in 1962. Against Johnson, Nixon, Ford, Carter, and

Reagan, he looks very good indeed. Besides, he was chosen in 1920 because he was handsome, affable, and bland, the perfect attributes for a media campaign.

CAMPAIGN SLOGAN: "Back to Normalcy"

PLATFORM*: Mr. Harding promises to oppose the League of Nations.
Mr. Harding promises arms limitation.
Mr. Harding promises to curb federal spending with a Bureau of the Budget.
Mr. Harding promises to pardon Eugene Debs after Woodrow Wilson's refusal to do so.
Mr. Harding promises to speak out for black rights in the South.
Mr. Harding promises tariff protection for American industry.

RUNNING MATE: Calvin Coolidge

SHADOW CABINET: Mr. Harding's cabinet will include Charles Evans Hughes, Andrew Mellon, Henry Wallace, Herbert Hoover, and Albert B. Fall. With the exception of Mr. Fall and Teapot Dome, the rest compare very well for ability with anything we have had lately.

PITFALL: A cad named Gaston Means said in 1930 that Flossie Harding poisoned her husband because he messed around with Carrie Phillips and Nan Britton and because he was in danger of being impeached. Flossie always was the brains and backbone of the duo. Most experts dismiss the accusation of Gaston Means, but the White House does not need another scandal—so a Harding reprise may be too big a gamble.

---

*While not as Lincolnesque as Al Jolson's campaign song insisted, this agenda looks pretty good compared to recent Republican platforms.

Gary Hart

EXPERIENCE: Mr. Hart was campaign manager for George McGovern in 1972. This is the equivalent of having been military strategist for General Custer at the Little Big Horn.

WINNABILITY: Quondam frontrunner Hart caught flak in 1984 for having changed his name and fibbed about his age. This time he quit rather peevishly when the Peeping Tom Brigade reported extramarital shenanigans. But women seem to find him appealing and men admire an old married guy who can get so much action, so against such dull-normal opponents Hart might still be drafted on the first ballot.

CAMPAIGN SLOGAN: "I'm No Womanizer—Go Ahead, Put a Tail on Me!"

PLATFORM: Mr. Hart promises that future indiscretions will be as discreet as those of FDR, Ike, JFK, and . . . well, come to think of it, JFK's indiscretions were pretty indiscreet, at that.
Mr. Hart promises that once he is President, he will finally talk about those new ideas he never got to talk about because of his name, his age, his lady friends, and so on.

RUNNING MATE: Andrew Greeley*

SHADOW CABINET: Press Secretary: The Unknown Comic
Secretary of State: Julio Iglesias

PITFALL: Mrs. Hart said she believed her husband when he said he spent the night with a gorgeous woman and nothing happened. If voters believe *that,* nobody will vote for Mr. Hart.

---

*Hey, the guy is sworn to celibacy, right?

Max Headroom

EXPERIENCE: Mr. Headroom is the ultimate deus ex machina. He is also the hottest thing on American television and in the Soda Pop Wars.

WINNABILITY: Mr. Headroom's ch-ch-charm is n-n-not necessarily easy to access. Older voters will not find him user-friendly. But young v-v-voters find he speaks their l-l-language. A guy who can get Ridley Scott to direct his commercials has got to be a threat in a media blitz.

CAMPAIGN SLOGAN:
"Don't Say the P Word!"

PLATFORM: Mr. Headroom promises to bring his bionic version of the phony bonhomie of Ted Baxter into the Oval Office. Mr. Headroom promises that after he cleans up Network 23, he will take on the American networks.

RUNNING MATE: C3PO

SHADOW CABINET: National Security Adviser: Peter Wagg
Secretary of State: Edison Carter
Press Secretary: Theora Jones
Inner Circle: George Stone, Rocky Morton, Annabelle Jankel

PITFALL: Mr. Headroom had cameo appearances by Jack Lemmon, Boy George, and Simon LeBon as proof of how truly hot he is, but *Batman* and *Miami Vice* enjoyed similar cult status at their peaks.

The track record of big-city mayors suggests that machine politicians who manipulate their images do better in local than national elections.

Jesse Helms

EXPERIENCE: Mr. Helms was the first Republican senator from North Carolina in this century. He has been in the Senate since 1972, and his seniority and his ideological consistency make him very influential.

WINNABILITY: When Mr. Helms ran the Tobacco Radio Network, he dismissed the civil rights movement as "contrived" and got college teacher Michael Paull suspended from the University of North Carolina for an assignment about Andrew Marvell's "To His Coy Mistress," which Mr. Helms considered obscene. Since then he has moved to the right.

CAMPAIGN SLOGAN: "To the Right, March!"

PLATFORM: Mr. Helms promises to support Taiwan as the only China.
Mr. Helms promises to fulfill Ronald Reagan's social agenda.
Mr. Helms promises to have more cash in his campaign war chest than the Treasury has in its coffers.

RUNNING MATE: Jesse James

SHADOW CABINET: Secretary of Transportation: Jessie Royce Landis
(The intriguing prospect of an all-Jesse administration is marred by the probability that famous Jesses like Jackson and Winchester would not be invited to join the Helms team.)

PITFALL: Mr. Helms has moved so far to the right that he is all but invisible from the center, and the candidate who holds the center will win the Presidency.

Hulk Hogan

EXPERIENCE: Mr. Hogan is heavyweight champion professional wrestler.

WINNABILITY: Mr. Hogan can certainly mop the floor with Paul Simon or Bob Dole or any of those lightweights. As for the general election, Mr. Hogan and the other candidates will draw straws or make some other sensible agreement beforehand to ensure Mr. Hogan's victory.

CAMPAIGN SLOGAN: "Hulkomania Is Sweeping the Nation"

PLATFORM: Mr. Hogan promises that the Senate will ratify treaties by Battle Royale, with all of the senators wearing those tiny trunks so their cheeks hang out. Mr. Hogan calls this Full Disclosure.
Mr. Hogan promises to shout at all enemies of the United States. He also promises to shout at all allies of the United States. In fact, he promises to shout on all occasions.
Mr. Hogan promises that fights between his line of dolls and G.I. Joe dolls will not be fixed.
Mr. Hogan promises to add the face of Gorgeous George to Mount Rushmore.

RUNNING MATE: Andre the Giant

SHADOW CABINET: Secretary of State: The Macho Man
Secretary of Transportation: The lovely Miss Elizabeth, manager of The Macho Man
Secretary of the Interior: The Killer Bees
Secretary of Education: George Steele

PITFALL: The Hulkster is a great favorite of the crowd, but as the last actor in the White House got mixed reviews the electorate may be ready to vote for an athlete.

Sherlock Holmes

EXPERIENCE: Mr. Holmes is a British confidential investigator who enjoyed some success against the Nazis in 1943's *Sherlock Holmes in Washington*.

WINNABILITY: In nearly 100 years only Irene Adler Norton bested Sherlock Holmes, and she is not expected to run against him.

CAMPAIGN SLOGAN: "The Game Is Afoot!"

PLATFORM: Mr. Holmes will handle scandals in Washington as discreetly as he did the scandal in Bohemia.
Mr. Holmes promises he can outwit the reds, even a whole red-headed league of them.

RUNNING MATE:
John Watson, M.D.

SHADOW CABINET: Secretary
of Defense: Mycroft Holmes
FBI Director: Inspector Lestrade
National Security Council:
Baker Street Irregulars
Secretary of the Interior:
Sigmund Freud

PITFALL: His use of cocaine could cost Mr. Holmes votes, even if it is only a seven-percent solution. He may also be *too* logical, like Jimmy Carter.

Dennis Hopper

EXPERIENCE: Mr. Hopper began his career as a thespian with an appearance on The Loretta Young Show in 1954.

WINNABILITY: Mr. Hopper was a rebel without a cause who took part in the gunfight at the OK Corral and wound up in the slammer with Cool Hand Luke and in *True Grit* with The Duke. As director and costar of *Easy Rider*, he was lionized at Cannes and became a cult hero all over the world even as his American career took a nosedive. A couple of years ago he suddenly started getting more work than anyone in his generation except maybe Richard Crenna or Dwayne Hickman. Voters love a sentimental comeback yarn.

CAMPAIGN SLOGAN: "Hop on the Hopper Bandwagon"

PLATFORM: Mr. Hopper promises to help fight the drug culture he did so much to create.

RUNNING MATE: Bobby Knight

SHADOW CABINET: Secretary of State: Gene Hackman
Ambassador to Italy: Francis Ford Coppola

PITFALL: In a campaign that considered Gary Hart too unconventional, Mr. Hopper may have the wrong image.

Lee Iacocca

EXPERIENCE: Mr. Iacocca earned a reputation as a marketing genius when he transformed Robert McNamara's dull Falcon into that "poor man's Thunderbird," the Mustang. Associates at Ford said after that, "Lee is like a Medici prince."

WINNABILITY: Medici prince or no Medici prince, Mr. Iacocca ran afoul of the papal infallibility of Henry Ford II and found himself at the head of a Chrysler Corporation on the edge of ruin. He begged for loan guarantees from the federal government. He worked for a dollar a year. Last year he was said to have earned more than $20 million. A guy who can multiply his salary by 20 million in a few years has got to know something about the economy.

CAMPAIGN SLOGAN: "Elect Chrysler's Imperial President"

PLATFORM: Mr. Iacocca promises to sublet the United States to the Japanese.
Mr. Iacocca promises to assemble the fleet of tall ships to sail up the Potomac for his inauguration.

RUNNING MATE: John DeLorean

SHADOW CABINET: Secretary of State: Lorenzo de' Medici
White House Chaplain: Pope Leo X

PITFALL: With the budget deficit the way it is, economists are not certain from whom Mr. Iacocca could beg massive loan guarantees next time around.

Jesse Jackson

EXPERIENCE: Mr. Jackson and a white youth were the best baseball players in their hometown, each getting contract offers from the New York Giants: the white was offered $95,000 and Mr. Jackson was offered $6,000. He decided to become a civil rights activist.

WINNABILITY: Mr. Jackson, candidate of the Rainbow Coalition, gave the best speeches in the 1984 campaign. Daniel Webster gave the best speeches in his heyday, too, only to see his Presidential aspirations go to the devil.

CAMPAIGN SLOGAN: "This Black Can Be Quarterback"*

PLATFORM: Mr. Jackson promises to complete the unfinished agenda of Martin Luther King.

RUNNING MATE: Bill Cosby**

SHADOW CABINET: White House Chaplain: Madalyn Murray

PITFALL: Voters who want to preserve the separation of church and state will be reluctant to support a clergyman even with the presence of the famous atheist as chaplain.

---

*When Mr. Jackson got to the University of Illinois on an athletic scholarship, the coach told him that blacks played the line, not quarterback, so he transferred to the Ag and Tech College of North Carolina at Greensboro, where he played quarterback.

**For twenty years Julian Bond was touted as the ideal black Vice President but his nasty divorce probably spells political oblivion for him, and may tarnish Andrew Young, too. That leaves Coz because.

Pope John Paul II

EXPERIENCE: Mr. II is administrative CEO of the world's 600 million or so Roman Catholics. He is also infallible on matters of faith and morals.

WINNABILITY: Mr. II has greater global name-recognition than anyone except Muhammad Ali. He is also the only peace candidate not cordially hated by the American right.

CAMPAIGN SLOGAN: "Solidarity Forever"

PLATFORM: Mr. II promises to be a President of all the people. Being fluent in Polish, Italian, English, French, German, and Spanish, he can talk just about everybody's language. He is also fluent in Latin in case the ghost of Julius Caesar haunts the White House.

RUNNING MATE: Albert Finney

SHADOW CABINET: Press Secretary: Andrej Jawien★
Secretary of State: Karol Wojtyla★★

PITFALL: Perhaps because he is so outspoken in favor of peace, Mr. II has been the target of several assassination attempts, prompting him to ride in a special bulletproof Popemobile. Voters will be reluctant to increase the danger of assassination by making him President, too.

★Andrej Jawien is the nom de plume of Karol Wojtyla.

★★Karol Wojtyla is the given name of Andrej Jawien.

Jack Kemp

EXPERIENCE: Mr. Kemp was quarterback for the Buffalo Bills.

WINNABILITY: Mr. Kemp looks like a former quarterback for the Buffalo Bills, and pundits like sports imagery so much that many voters think of the President as the quarterback of America's team. This means Roger Staubach has more winnability than Mr. Kemp, but Roger Staubach tarnished his all-American image as a shill and that makes Mr. Kemp the only quarterback in the race.

CAMPAIGN SLOGAN: "Kemp Can Beat the Russkies with the Long Bomb"

PLATFORM: Mr. Kemp promises less snow for Buffalo.
Mr. Kemp promises to simplify taxes by having the rich pay no taxes and the poor collect no benefits. Simple, eh?

RUNNING MATE: "Buffalo" Roth

SHADOW CABINET: Secretary of Defense: Buffalo Bill
Secretary of Education: Buffalo Bob
School Lunch: Buffalo Chips
National Security Council: Buffalo Sabres

PITFALL: We have already had a President from Buffalo: he won the popular vote in 1884, 1888, and 1892, and he won the electoral college in 1884 and 1892. Grover Cleveland was a hefty man with intelligence, integrity, and an illegitimate child. Grover Cleveland could never win today. A fat guy from Buffalo with a bastard brat? Television would make short work of Grover Cleveland, and NFL or no NFL, Jack Kemp is not in a league with Grover Cleveland.

Adnan Khashoggi

EXPERIENCE: Mr. Khashoggi may not be the richest man in the world, but he is the one who most conspicuously personifies the vulgar fantasies of high living harbored by every schnook who ever bought a lottery ticket.

WINNABILITY: P. T. Barnum said nobody ever went broke by overestimating the vulgarity of the American public, and the garish life-style of Khashoggi, the reputed model for the title character in Harold Robbins's 1974 novel *The Pirate*, will certainly appeal to many voters.

CAMPAIGN SLOGAN: "AK All the Way"

PLATFORM: Mr. Khashoggi, who was once sued for $2.5 billion during his California divorce, promises to abolish alimony.
Mr. Khashoggi promises to redecorate Air Force One after the fashion of his sybaritic DC-8 with its $200,000 Russian sable bedspread.
Mr. Khashoggi promises to let the press corps use his family nickname, "Baba," during press conferences.
Mr. Khashoggi promises to let Franco Nero, star of the movie version of *The Pirate*, sit-in for him at Presidential photo opportunities.

RUNNING MATE: Jacqueline Onassis

SHADOW CABINET: Secretary of State: Sheik Yamani
Director of the National Security Council: John Poindexter
Ambassador to Israel: Jonathan Pollard

PITFALL: Mr. Khashoggi was middleman in the Iranscam contragate arms-for-hostages swap with Iran that went sour. Some of his real estate deals in Salt Lake City look pretty sour at the moment, too. Voters may suspect that Mr. Khashoggi is losing his Midas touch.

Ed Koch

EXPERIENCE: Mr. Koch is the mayor of New York; he is the only mayor with his own foreign policy. He is also the only mayor who has appeared in a Muppet movie.

WINNABILITY: In New York, the I's have it—the Italians, the Israelis, and the Irish. Mr. Koch has cultivated these groups so effectively he is nicknamed Ethnic Ed. The I's provide a pretty fair political base.

CAMPAIGN SLOGAN: "How'm I Doin'?"

PLATFORM: Mr. Koch promises to atone for his liberal beginnings by becoming more conservative than Senator Daniel Patrick Moynihan.

Mr. Koch promises a free copy of his autobiography, *Mayor,* for every library that burns a copy of the unauthorized biography *I, Koch.*

RUNNING MATE: Bunny Persky Grossinger

SHADOW CABINET: White House Chief of Staff: David Garth
Secretary of Commerce:
Bess Myerson

PITFALL: Mr. Koch's quips make wonderful copy but he seems to be evolving from colorful eccentricity through egomania toward solipsism. No mayor of New York has ever won higher office and it does not look like Mr. Koch will break that jinx.

Dr. C. Everett Koop

EXPERIENCE: Dr. Koop is Surgeon General of the United States.

WINNABILITY: Although most of his predecessors ignored the option and dressed in mufti, the surgeon general is entitled to military rank. Dr. Koop likes to dress in full military regalia, not just on ceremonial occasions but whenever he is at the office or shopping at the mall or stopping by the fast-food franchise for a bag of burgers. The large man looks very distinguished in his dress uniform, just like the kind of President most voters want.

CAMPAIGN SLOGAN: "Safe Sex Is Better than Slow Death"

PLATFORM: Dr. Koop promises to urge celibacy on all school-children.
Dr. Koop promises to provide condoms to all schoolchildren because he believes the Second Coming will arrive before the kids take to celibacy in a really big way.

RUNNING MATE: Dr. Benjamin Spock

SHADOW CABINET: Secretary of State: Dr. James Kildare
Secretary of Agriculture: Dr. Galen Adams
Secretary of Defense: Dr. Marcus Welby
Director of the Drug Enforcement Agency: Dr. K

PITFALL: Dr. Koop is said to be a born-again Christian. If he gets born *again*, or even if his last rebirth took place since 1954, he will be too young to assume the Presidency, under the constitutional requirement of thirty-five.

Lyndon LaRouche, Jr.

EXPERIENCE: Lyndon LaRouche lives like a king but pays no taxes. In this, at least, Mr. LaRouche exemplifies a favorite American fantasy.

WINNABILITY: Mr. LaRouchies says that Queen Elizabeth II is a notorious smuggler of illicit drugs. In fact, the queen's luggage was found to contain marijuana when she left Canada but everyone suspects it was planted there by a wacko provincial premier and not by Her Majesty. Still, twisting the lion's tail has always been a way to court the Irish vote.

CAMPAIGN SLOGAN: "LaRouche Is the Most Inspirational Leader Since L. Ron Hubbard"

PLATFORM: Mr. LaRouche would make AIDS carriers clang bells like the lepers of old.

RUNNING MATE: Martin Bormann

SHADOW CABINET: White House Chaplain: The Reverend Jim Jones
Ambassador to France: Klaus Barbie, "The Butcher of Lyons"
National Security Council: The Aryan Nation

PITFALL: A couple of LaRouchies snuck onto the ballot in Illinois because nobody knew what they stood for, but the chances of LaRouche himself are reckoned by oddsmakers as slightly less than those of a snowball in hell. (Besides, we had a President named Lyndon and it just didn't work out.)

Robin Leach

EXPERIENCE: Mr. Leech . . . whoops, make that Mr. Leach is the charming cockney whose adenoidal cheerleading for the sybaritic vulgarity of the rich and famous is making *him* rich and famous. He gushes alliterative observations along the lines of: "In this beautiful baronial baroque bathroom each roll of baby-blue bumfluff costs *Four Thousand Dollars!*"

WINNABILITY: The tenacious toadying of the affable Mr. Leach has such widespread appeal among materialistic voyeurs that the profile of him on ABC's *20/20* was as hagiographic as his profiles of the monied elite. Mr. Leach is plugged into the fantasies of every voter who ever daydreamed while buying a lottery ticket.

CAMPAIGN SLOGAN: "You Are What You Own"

PLATFORM: Mr. Leach promises that he will bring the tabloid style of the *National Enquirer* and the *Star* to 1600 Pennsylvania Avenue as he has brought it to the home screen.
Mr. Leach promises that his administration will do nothing to ruffle the feathers of any voter with more than $50 million.

RUNNING MATE: Phineas T. Barnum

SHADOW CABINET: Secretary of the Treasury: Michael Anthony*

PITFALL: The criminal shenanigans of public officials and Wall Street movers and shakers may make voters ask not how much money a person has but how the money was obtained. A killjoy question like that could cause a bear market for megamaterialism.

---

*Michael Anthony was the personal secretary of eccentric billionaire John Beresford Tipton, the guy whose idea of a gag was to give strangers a million bucks.

Huey Pierce Long

EXPERIENCE: Mr. Long was governor of and then senator from Louisiana.

WINNABILITY: Mr. Long had great support in Louisiana and around the nation because many voters believed him when he said he wanted to help the poor.

CAMPAIGN SLOGAN: "Vote for the Kingfish"

PLATFORM: Mr. Long promises to "Share the Wealth" with a guaranteed annual income, a cap on personal income at $1 million, and an inheritance tax that allows only $3 million to be passed to beneficiaries in a will.

RUNNING MATE: Moon Landrieu*

SHADOW CABINET: Secretary of State: Broderick Crawford
Press Secretary: John Ireland
Attorney General: Russell Long
National Security Adviser: John Derek
Secretary of Transportation: Mercedes McCambridge

PITFALL: Mr. Long's Share the Wealth plan is so radical it could get him shot. Nicknamed "Kingfish" (for "undisputed master") by his fans, he risks confusion with George Stevens, "Kingfish" at the Mystic Knights of the Sea Lodge (*not* the George Stevens who won an Oscar for *A Place in the Sun*).

---

*Except for coming from Louisiana, Moon Landrieu has little in common with Huey Long, but his name is so wonderful it belongs on a ticket.

Ronald McDonald

EXPERIENCE: Mr. McDonald is a clown.

WINNABILITY: Mr. McDonald is known for his charitable endeavors.
Many voters say to themselves a year after an election, "To think I voted for that clown!" Mr. McDonald should be able to form a coalition of clown voters.

CAMPAIGN SLOGAN: "McVote for McMe"

PLATFORM: Mr. McDonald promises to do it his way (it's the other guys who promise to do it your way).

RUNNING MATE: Seven Ann McDonald★

SHADOW CABINET: Secretary of War: General George McClellan
Secretary of Agriculture: Cyrus McCormick
Secretary of Education: William Holmes McGuffey
Librarian of Congress: Claude McKay
Presidential Speechwriter: Mary McCarthy
National Security Council: John McGraw, Doug McClure, Mary Margaret McBride, Joel McCrea, Frank McHugh, Roddy McDowall, David McCallum, Patrick McGoohan, Kristy McNichol, and Marion McPartland
Ambassador from Scotland: Macbeth

PITFALL: Voters may worry that Mr. McDonald would add golden arches to the American flag.

★Seven Ann McDonald played Jennie, the precocious brat on *The Eddie Capra Mysteries*. (*Now* you remember!)

Spuds MacKenzie

EXPERIENCE: Mr. MacKenzie is the canine corporate logo for Budweiser light beer.

WINNABILITY: As the ultimate party animal, Mr. MacKenzie might appeal to an electorate that was very fond of Ike, a President who spent most of his time playing golf. Presidents since Ike have proven less successful, even when given to naps. A cheerful party animal might be just what the nation needs.

CAMPAIGN SLOGAN: "Party! Party! Party!"

PLATFORM: Mr. MacKenzie promises a constitutional amendment banning hangovers.
Mr. MacKenzie promises to improve the quality of American television by replacing over-the-hill jocks with cute little animals in beer ads.

RUNNING MATE: Victor, the RCA dog

SHADOW CABINET: Secretary of State: Morris the Cat
Press Secretary: Mr. Ed
Secretary of Defense: Francis the Talking Mule
National Security Adviser: Bonzo

PITFALL: Mr. MacKenzie is always shown in the company of very attractive young women who seem engaged in frenetic efforts to prove Cyndi Lauper correct that girls just want to have fun. This behavior pattern scuttled the candidacy of Gary Hart, and could jeopardize the viability of Mr. MacKenzie's campaign as well.

Shirley MacLaine

EXPERIENCE: Ms. MacLaine lived the favorite fantasy in the world, the one from *42nd Street,* in which understudy Ruby Keeler became a star overnight. Ms. MacLaine was understudy to Carol Haney in *Pajama Game* in 1954 when the star broke her ankle.

WINNABILITY: The charming Ms. MacLaine is as likable a celebrity as any in the land. She supported Adlai, JFK, Bobby K, and George McGovern. She tried to save Caryl Chessman from the gas chamber and made a documentary about Red China. She's a voracious reader; Ernie Kovacs said that if you had her for a friend, you wouldn't need an encyclopedia. Talented, adorable, earnest, she ought to be as popular with voters as Irma La Douce was with her fans.

CAMPAIGN SLOGAN: "Don't Fall off the Mountain"

PLATFORM: Ms. MacLaine promises to find out the trouble with Harry.
Ms. MacLaine promises to know the turning point.

RUNNING MATE: Jack Lemmon

SHADOW CABINET: Press Secretary: Shirley Logan

PITFALL: Ms. MacLaine believes in reincarnation. She *really* believes in it, enough to go out on a limb. Voters who like her in this incarnation may worry about who she might have been down through the ages.

Ed McMahon

EXPERIENCE: Mr. McMahon began as a carney mike-man for Bingo, became the clown on TV's *The Big Top* whose red nose flashed hello, and ended up as the guy who mails you those multi-million-dollar sweepstakes forms. Oh yeah . . . you may have seen him on *The Tonight Show.*

WINNABILITY: Mr. McMahon's role as foil to quipster Johnny Carson is to embody the Ordinary Guy, the good-natured Everyman whose sturdy dependability proves that nobody need be offended by any of the gags. As fighter pilot, huckster, and Good Old Boy, Mr. McMahon is a dream candidate.

CAMPAIGN SLOGAN: "And Now Heeeeeeeeeeeeeere's . . . *Eddie!*"

PLATFORM: Mr. McMahon promises not to drink on the job any more often than Richard Nixon or Franklin Pierce.
Mr. McMahon promises to play Who Do You Trust? with the Russians.

RUNNING MATE: Horace McMahon*

SHADOW CABINET: Ambassador to Nepal: Joan Rivers

PITFALL: As the perfect second banana, Mr. McMahon may have trouble getting voters to accept him as Top Banana. Everyone knows that the Top Banana is Phil Silvers.

---

*Tsk tsk, how fleeting is fame. Horace McMahon was the steely-eyed hard-nosed Lieutenant Mike Parker who gave *Naked City* its aura.

Madonna

EXPERIENCE: Ms. Madonna is a much-maligned superstar who calls herself a "hyperactive adult."

WINNABILITY: The women's movement has been ambivalent about Madonna because she is so blatantly sexy with her Boy Toy buckle on her unchastity belt. She manipulates the media better than anybody since Teddy Roosevelt, though, which is more important than a few captious critics who call her a "tarted-up sex kitten" with a "kitchy-koo" voice.

CAMPAIGN SLOGAN: "Desperately Seeking the White House"

PLATFORM: Ms. Madonna promises to be a Material President who knows that the campaign contributor with the cold hard cash is always Mr. Right.
Ms. Madonna promises to handle foreign policy like a virgin.
Ms. Madonna promises there will be no more Shanghai surprises.

RUNNING MATE: Louise Veronica Ciccone

SHADOW CABINET: Secretary of Defense: Sean Penn
Secretary of Education: Cyndi Lauper

PITFALL: Ms. Madonna is currently the ubiquitous icon of pop culture. By Election Day she could be a minor deity like Moon Unit Zappa or Brooke Shields.

Steve Martin

EXPERIENCE: Mr. Martin is the quondam philosophy student who became a crazy kinda guy, a ramblin' kinda guy, a yew-neek kinda guy, and even a lonely guy.

WINNABILITY: Mr. Martin considers politics "a depressing subject" and keeps his humor apolitical. Many voters agree that politics is depressing. They might support a guy who plays the banjo and tap dances to make them smile.

CAMPAIGN SLOGAN: "I Forgot!"

PLATFORM: Mr. Martin will handle all foreign policy blunders by saying, "Ex-cuuuuuuuuuuuuuuuuse me!"
Mr. Martin will not wear plaid.

RUNNING MATE: Bernadette Peters

SHADOW CABINET: Secretary of State: Pat Paulsen
Secretary of Education: Tom Smothers
Éminence grise: Carl Reiner

PITFALL: Remembering Mr. Martin with an arrow through his head, the electorate may decide it does not want to send a jerk off to the White House except in the traditional way—by mistake.

Groucho Marx

EXPERIENCE: Mr. Marx is the acknowledged master of that quintessentially American art form, the wisecrack. His executive experience includes a term as president of Huxley College and as king of Freedonia.

WINNABILITY: If Mr. Marx can prevent his managers from interrupting his madcap antics with banal songs and inane plots, he can be irresistible.

CAMPAIGN SLOGAN: "You Bet Your Life"

PLATFORM: Mr. Marx promises to build a viaduct.*
Mr. Marx promises to establish trade balance with Japan, drawing on his experience as Koko in NBC's 1960 *Mikado*.
Mr. Marx promises to award the Medal of Freedom to Lydia the Tattooed Lady.

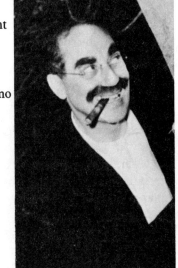

RUNNING MATE: Margaret Dumont

SHADOW CABINET:
Press Secretary: Harpo
White House Chief of Staff: Gummo
Chief of Protocol: Zeppo
All other posts bar none: Chico

PITFALL: The surrealistic satire of Mr. Marx and his siblings, however nostalgic in retrospect, is out of synch with the bland humor of the eighties.

*Why a viaduct? Don't ask!

Edwin Meese III

EXPERIENCE: Edwin Meese made his name by attacking the free speech movement at Berkeley in 1964 when he was a deputy district attorney. He became an aide to Governor Ronald Reagan in 1967.

WINNABILITY: Mr. Meese is the closest adviser to President Reagan. While pundits hint that Nancy or Howard Baker call the shots, it is Mr. Meese who is top dog. Voters who wish to sustain the Reagan Revolution should prefer Mr. Meese to any other candidate. Mr. Reagan has called him an alter ego.

CAMPAIGN SLOGAN: "Law and Order . . . Especially Order"

PLATFORM: Mr. Meese promises to ignore amendments to the Constitution so he can focus on what the Founding Fathers *really* wanted.
Mr. Meese promises not to offend the apartheid regime in South Africa so American women will not have to do without jewelry.
Mr. Meese will balance the budget by taxing the unemployed.

RUNNING MATE: Rudolph Giuliani

SHADOW CABINET: Mr. Meese will stick with the Reagan team during his first term. It will take some time to make decisions for himself.

PITFALL: Mr. Meese called the American Civil Liberties Union part of a nationwide "criminals' lobby." With so many on Wall Street facing trial, even Republicans may find Mr. Meese soft on civil rights.

John Stuart Mill

EXPERIENCE: Mr. Mill is the Father of Liberalism.

WINNABILITY: Liberalism is so weak in the United States that only its father might admit to being liberal without immediately saying "but," as in: "I'm liberal on civil rights but it's time for benign neglect" or "I'm liberal on women's rights but who is going to raise the kids?" or "I'm liberal on labor relations but I hate unions." Teddy Kennedy has lost forty pounds but he hasn't lost Chappaquiddick or his ill-fated attempt to deny the nomination to an incumbent President, a trick not even managed by Teddy Roosevelt in 1912. Mr. Mill is liberalism's only hope.

CAMPAIGN SLOGAN: "Down by the Old Mill's Dream"

PLATFORM: Mr. Mill promises to question all things; to turn away from no difficulty; to accept no doctrine without rigid scrutiny; to let no fallacy step by unperceived; to insist upon knowing the meaning of a word before using it and the meaning of a proposition before assenting to it.

RUNNING MATE: I. F. Stone*

SHADOW CABINET: Secretary of Commerce: Ralph Nader
Press Secretary: Charlayne Hunter-Gault
Secretary of Defense: Günter Grass**

PITFALL: The FCC has only seven dirty words, but politics in the eighties has eight and the eighth is *liberal*.

---

*Izzy Stone is not only a liberal's liberal, he gives us the Mill/Stone ticket.

**Mr. Grass suggested universal military training in guerrilla warfare tactics to make a nation invasion-proof without giving it the imperial capacity to bully its neighbors, a liberal compromise between a nuclear first-strike strategy and unilateral disarmament.

Mother Teresa

EXPERIENCE: Mother Teresa is a Roman Catholic nun of the Congregation of the Missionaries of Charity. She founded the Nirmal Hriday ("Pure Heart") Home for Dying Destitutes in Calcutta in 1952. There are *a lot* of dying destitutes in Calcutta. Her work with them and with other outcasts including American AIDS victims convinces many people, atheists included, that the woman is a saint.

WINNABILITY: Well, it might be a big mistake to bet against her. Besides the possibility of pull with The Man Upstairs, this woman whose serenity and goodness fortify her colleagues is also tough, alert, unsentimental, and charismatic. While other religious orders languish to or past the point of extinction, hers is growing.

CAMPAIGN SLOGAN: "Something Beautiful for God and Man"

PLATFORM: Mother Teresa promises to be tolerant of everyone, even political activists like the Berrigan Boys, of whom she said, "If they feel this is the way they must serve Him, that is between them and God."
Mother Teresa will work for peace with no illusions—her 1971 visit to Belfast, where she talked with Ian Paisley, produced no miracle. Maybe her next visit will.

RUNNING MATE: Mother Cabrini

SHADOW CABINET: The Sisters of Loreto and The Boomtown Rats

PITFALL: Even the luckiest President of them all had his Teflon tarnished in the rough-and-tumble of Presidential politics. The world has only one saint-by-consensus. She is quite simply too good for the job.

Eddie Murphy

EXPERIENCE: Mr. Murphy has experience in law enforcement in Beverly Hills.

WINNABILITY: Mr. Murphy may be the first graduate of *Saturday Night Live* to fulfill the potential demonstrated on the small screen. He is so likable he gets laughs for material as sprinkled with expletives as the Nixon tapes. He might have trouble carrying parts of the rural South because he is so closely identified with New York City and Los Angeles. As a Murphy, he should easily carry the Irish vote.

CAMPAIGN SLOGAN: "Get Ready for Eddie"

PLATFORM: Mr. Murphy promises to resolve all crises within forty-eight hours.

RUNNING MATE: Richard Pryor

SHADOW CABINET:
FBI Director: Nick Nolte
Economic Advisers: Don Ameche
and Ralph Bellamy
Speechwriters: Freeman Gosden
and Charles Correll
Press Secretary: Geraldine Jones*

*Ms. Jones will need permission from
her boyfriend, Killer.

PITFALL: Mr. Murphy would risk millions by running because of the equal-time provisions that kept *Bedtime for Bonzo* off the airwaves during the 1980 and 1984 campaigns. It is intriguing to imagine the mainstream politicians trying to top his live specials for the cable networks.

Yasuhiro Nakasone

EXPERIENCE: Mr. Nakasone is Prime Minister of Japan.

WINNABILITY: Voters who fret that the American economy is not competitive enough should respond well to the leader of an economy that is.

CAMPAIGN SLOGAN: "Forget Pearl Harbor"

PLATFORM: Mr. Nakasone promises to revitalize the American economy by retraining technologically unemployed workers to manufacture the Ronson lighter.
Mr. Nakasone promises to include the United States in the Far East Asian Co-Prosperity Sphere.
Mr. Nakasone promises that government officials who dishonor themselves will be expected to commit hara-kiri.

RUNNING MATE: Tokyo Rose

SHADOW CABINET: Instead of a cabinet, Mr. Nakasone's administration will be run by MITI, the Ministry of International Trade and Industry, the phenomenally successful brain trust that American businessmen instinctively mistrust and admire.

PITFALL: Americans have been taught for over a century to mistrust the very notion of a planned economy. Our unplanned economy may have to sink much deeper into chaos and mediocrity before that faith is shaken.

Jack Nicholson

EXPERIENCE: Mr. Nicholson began by starring in *The Little Shop of Horrors,* a cult film that finally came full circle to enjoy a new vogue as camp classic. *That's* staying power!

WINNABILITY: Face it, the electorate would vote for anybody to get the magnificent Anjelica Huston as First Lady. This guy is unbeatable.

CAMPAIGN SLOGAN: "Elect an Easy Rider"

PLATFORM: Mr. Nicholson promises to investigate the water scandals in Los Angeles, even at the risk of getting his nose slit.
Mr. Nicholson promises the Oval Office will be no crazier than a cuckoo's nest.

RUNNING MATE: Catman Scrothers

SHADOW CABINET: Press Secretary: Big Nurse
Ambassador to Moscow: Warren Beatty
National Security Council: Jane Fonda, Peter Fonda, and Dennis Hopper

PITFALL: Mr. Nicholson goes *waaaaaaay* back to the fifties when cool was cool was cool, and Mr. Nicholson has no rival as King of Cool among honkie superstars. No real cool cat would risk such an august status for a mere Presidency, making it unlikely that Mr. Nicholson would stoop to so dubious a conquest.

Lieutenant Colonel Oliver North

EXPERIENCE: Mr. North has conducted his very own personal foreign policy. Once he supposedly called a Central American head of state, Costa Rican President Oscar Arias, threatening to cut off $80 million in aid unless Arias scrubbed a scheduled press conference announcing a clandestine contra airfield in Costa Rica. This is a guy who knows how to cut red tape!

WINNABILITY: When it seemed obvious that North had broken the law and ignored the Constitution, the President called him a "national hero"; when he appeared on The Hill, lawmakers fell all over themselves to sing his praises and have their pictures taken with him in his Marine uniform.

CAMPAIGN SLOGAN: "We Want Ollie, by Golly!"

PLATFORM: Mr. North promises to eliminate—not reduce, *eliminate*—the Pentagon budget by privatizing it as he did with the contra defense budget: under the North administration, all American armaments would be paid for by super-rich patriots giving voluntarily.

Mr. North promises to deliver inscribed Bibles to all Arab leaders along with little lectures sprinkled with scriptural aphorisms.

Mr. North promises to take the Fifth at press conferences unless reporters grant him limited immunity.

RUNNING MATE: Eugene Hasenfus

SHADOW CABINET: Secretary of State: Manucher Ghorbanifar*
Attorney General: Theodore Shackley**
National Security Adviser: John Poindexter***

PITFALL: People have been so fascinated by the colorful she-nanigans that they seem to have missed some key points, such as that Mr. North made a botch of things. If it comes out that he diverted cash from his slush funds into Congressional elections or that his contra buddies were in the drug trade, his heroic image might be tarnished.

Dolly Parton

EXPERIENCE: Ms. Parton is the pop superstar who crossed over from country-western music into the mainstream, where she epito-mizes jet-set chic. Her 1977 New York opening drew Mick Jagger, Bruce Springsteen, Andy Warhol, and Phoebe Snow.

WINNABILITY: Anybody who can appeal to the Nashville set *and* the *Vogue* crowd has got to be able to get votes from across the political spectrum.

CAMPAIGN SLOGAN: "Whatever Happens, Dolly Will Put Up a Good Front"

*Ghorbanifar is the Iranian businessman who said Iranscam was a humanitarian tractors-for-hostages deal.

**Shackley is the CIA vet who, understandably, wanted to spring his buddy William Buckley, CIA station chief in Beirut who was taken hostage.

***Poindexter told North "Well done" for lying to the House Intelligence Committee.

72

PLATFORM: Ms. Parton promises equal opportunity for secretaries. Ms. Parton promises equal opportunity for short people. Ms. Parton promises to bring the variety show back to prime time, even if she does seem miscast as the Ed Sullivan of the late eighties.

RUNNING MATE: Porter Wagoner

SHADOW CABINET: Secretary of State: Brenda Lee National Security Council: The Mandrell sisters Secretary of Education: Tammy Wynette Ambassador to Lebanon: Dabney Coleman

PITFALL: *The New York Times* spoke of Ms. Parton's "almost fervent sincerity." American voters may not be ready for a President with "almost fervent sincerity."

Nancy Reagan

EXPERIENCE: The First Lady ran the nation from the time she replaced Donald Regan with Howard Baker, perhaps before, becoming the second "Lady President," the first having been Edith Wilson, who ran the nation for over a year after her husband Woodrow's stroke on October 2, 1919.

WINNABILITY: As Nancy Davis, she first costarred with Ronald Reagan on February 5, 1953, in a *Ford Theater* teleplay called *First Born*. She and Ron did *Money and the Minister* for *General Electric*

Theater and costarred in the 1957 movie *Hellcats of the Navy*. It was acting in such things that gave her husband his winnability and it is only fair that voters would be as generous to her.

CAMPAIGN SLOGAN: "Let Nancy Be Nancy"

PLATFORM: Mrs. Reagan, who packs a pistol in her handbag, will provide handguns to the wives of all public officials so they can shoot it out with troublemakers.
Mrs. Reagan promises to buy new dishes for the White House, the old ones having gotten chipped and tacky after *eight years* of use.

RUNNING MATE: Jane Wyman

SHADOW CABINET: National Security Adviser: Jeane Kirkpatrick
Press Secretary: Maureen Reagan
Attorneys General: Cheech and Chong

PITFALL: One former Reagan aide described the First Lady as a "bulldog" and said that putting up with her required the "patience of Job." The American electorate is long-suffering, but Job-like it ain't.

Ronald Reagan

EXPERIENCE: Mr. Reagan costarred in *Hellcats of the Navy* with Nancy Davis.

WINNABILITY: Oh, he has the winnability, all right!

CAMPAIGN SLOGAN: "A Third Term for the Gipper!"

PLATFORM: Mr. Reagan promises to balance the budget by a combination of tax cuts and reductions in domestic spending.
Mr. Reagan promises to spend so much money on defense that the Russians will go broke trying to keep pace with our arms buildup.

RUNNING MATE: George Bush

SHADOW CABINET: Secretary of State: Alexander Haig
National Security Adviser: Richard Allen
(That's right, you get the gag—everybody who quit in dudgeon, disgrace, or both, from Admiral Poindexter to Don Regan.)

PITFALL: Ronald Reagan is prohibited by the Twenty-second Amendment from running for a third term. However, his attorney general, Ed Meese, has been telling people that amendments are not the real Constitution but only *amendments*, after all, and not even the real Constitution prevented the administration from, say, mining the waters of Nicaragua or funding the contras in violation of the Boland Amendment.

Pat Robertson

EXPERIENCE: Mr. Robertson is a TV evangelist who did not get blackmailed in a sex scandal or blackmail his viewers with death threats from On High. This makes him a middle-of-the-road media evangelist, about halfway between the tradition of Aimee Semple McPherson and that of Father Coughlin.

WINNABILITY: Mr. Robertson has the endorsement of Roy Rogers and Dale Evans.

CAMPAIGN SLOGAN: "Somebody Up There Likes Me"

PLATFORM: Mr. Robertson promises to balance the budget by having Oral Roberts raise millions upon millions from people who do not want God to strike Oral dead, and by raising millions more from those of the opposite persuasion.
Mr. Robertson promises to have prayer in the schools, between the geography classes about the flat earth and the biology classes based on the Book of Genesis.

RUNNING MATE: Oral Roberts

SHADOW CABINET: Secretary of the Treasury: Archbishop Paul Marcinkus *
Secretary of Agriculture: Jimmy Swaggart
Secretary of State: Billy Sunday
Press Secretary: Elmer Gantry

PITFALL: When Oral Roberts had just gotten the $1.3 million he needed to avoid sudden death at the hands of an Angry God, thanks to the pious owner of that Florida dog track, he decided to broadcast his support for Jimmy and Tammy Faye in their hour of need when . . . *Crash!* A thunderbolt put him off the air. Maybe Somebody Up There is getting tired of people shilling in His name.

Tom Selleck

EXPERIENCE: Mr. Selleck went to USC on an athletic scholarship and Mickey Mantle thought he could play in the majors, but instead Selleck became a contestant on *The Dating Game* (he did *not* get the girl) and a stud in the Gore Vidal/Mae West disaster *Myra Breckinridge*. Oh yeah, he played a car dealer in *Daughters of Satan* and a hunk on *The Young and the Restless*.

WINNABILITY: As the "Clark Gable of the eighties," the conservative Mr. Selleck—he supports Ronald Reagan and reads *The National Review*—would be a very effective campaigner. His self-deprecating humor disarms potential male jealousy, and it is hard to imagine anyone getting more votes from women.

CAMPAIGN SLOGAN: "Send a P.I. to D.C."

---

*This will be an ecumenical administration dedicated to the proposition that you do not have to be born again to find allure in big bucks.

PLATFORM: Mr. Magnum . . . excuse me, Mr. Selleck promises that his politics will always take the high road (except to China). Mr. Magnum promises . . . whoops, make that Mr. Selleck promises that his President will be as perfect as Lance White on *The Rockford Files*.

RUNNING MATE: Jack Lord

SHADOW CABINET:
Secretary of State: Robert Conrad
Secretary of Defense: Anthony Eisley
Secretary of the Interior: Poncie Ponce
Secretary: Connie Stevens *

PITFALL: Before the most recent renewal of *Magnum, P.I.*, they made a supposed "final episode" with Mr. Selleck wandering around as the ghost of his character, only to have to bring him back like Bobby on *Dallas*. For dying and then not staying dead, Mr. Selleck may strike voters as indecisive.

William Shatner

EXPERIENCE: Mr. Shatner plays T. J. Hooker and hosted *Saturday Night Live*. He was Jeff Cable on *The Barbary Coast* and Ralph Bellamy's son who defended Steve McQueen on the 1957 *Studio One* episode "The Defender," which became the series *The Defenders*.

* That is, the cast of the original detective show from Hawaii, *Hawaiian Eye*.

WINNABILITY: Mr. Shatner played the WASP captain of the ethnic crew on the starship *Enterprise*. From MGM bomber crews to *Voyage to the Bottom of the Sea,* there is always a WASP captain and an ethnic crew. The establishment fantasy is that no matter how small a minority they become, the WASPs will always provide the captains.

CAMPAIGN SLOGAN: "Beam Me Up, Scotty—There's No Intelligent Life in Congress"

PLATFORM: Mr. Shatner promises to boldly go where no man has gone before.
Mr. Shatner promises to boldly split infinitives no matter who writes his speeches.
Mr. Shatner promises to fix the trouble with Tribbles.

RUNNING MATE: Leonard Nimoy

SHADOW CABINET: Surgeon General: DeForest Kelley
Ambassador to Moscow: Walter Koenig
Secretary of State: Richard Coogan*

*Mr. Coogan was the original Captain Video, whose Video Rangers fought to save planet Earth from Mook the Moon Man, Kul of Eos, Dr. Clysmok, and the evil Astroidal Society under Hal Conklin's Dr. Pauli.

PITFALL: Mr. Shatner told the Trekkies to grow up when he hosted *Saturday Night Live*. If they do, his fanatical core of support will evaporate.

Paul Simon

EXPERIENCE: Mr. Simon is either the Democratic senator from Illinois or a pop superstar. (Or both—have they ever been seen together?)

WINNABILITY: Mr. Simon is either an expert on Abraham Lincoln or the star of *One Trick Pony*.

CAMPAIGN SLOGAN: "We've All Come to Look for America"

PLATFORM: Mr. Simon promises to teach the United Nations that helping to make Ladysmith Black Mambazu into international celebrities is not a clever ploy in support of apartheid.
Mr. Simon promises to teach Americans how to get rich selling real estate.*

RUNNING MATE: Art Garfunkel**

SHADOW CABINET: Secretary of the Treasury: William Simon
Press Secretary: Neil Simon
Secretary of Defense: Carly Simon
Attorney General: Simple Simon
CIA Director: Simon Templar

PITFALL: The Paul Simon who squeaked past Charles Percy to criticize Reaganomics in the Senate is cute but not cute enough to have stolen Annie Hall from Woody Allen.

---

*Wait a minute, how many identities does this guy have?

**Art Garfunkel is the perfect running mate for any of the Paul Simons. In fact, Art Garfunkel has the perfect karma to be running mate for any candidate.

Bruce Springsteen

EXPERIENCE: In "We Are the World," Mr. Springsteen had one of the few voices you could recognize before some other voice you didn't quite recognize butted in.

WINNABILITY: Mr. Springsteen would easily carry the youth vote, the blue-collar vote, the women's vote, and New Jersey. It is time for The Boss to be *The Boss!*

CAMPAIGN SLOGAN: "Born in the USA"

PLATFORM: Mr. Springsteen promises Chrysler-like federal loan guarantees to subsidize the production of pink Cadillacs.
Mr. Springsteen promises executive clemency for Johnny 99.
Just as he improved "Santa Claus Is Coming to Town" with a rock version, Mr. Springsteen promises a rock version of "Hail to the Chief" entitled "Hail to the Boss."

RUNNING MATE: Tina Turner

SHADOW CABINET: Secretary of State: Little Steven
Secretary of Defense: Joan Baez
Secretary of Education: Twisted Sister
National Security Council: The E Street Band

PITFALL: Many of the airheads at Springsteen concerts waving flags during "Born in the USA" seem to think he is the musical equivalent of Rambo. If they listen to his songs and discover that he is intelligent and poetic, he will lose their votes. The last intelligent and poetic candidate was Eugene McCarthy and everyone knows what happened to him. (Whatever *did* happen to Eugene McCarthy, anyway?)

Sylvester Stallone

EXPERIENCE: Mr. Stallone began as a Lord of Flatbush before evolving through several Rockies into Rambo.

WINNABILITY: Mr. Stallone shares with Charlie Chaplin and Orson Welles the honor of having been nominated for Academy Awards in both the Best Actor and the Best Screenwriter categories. Pauline Kael compared him to Marlon Brando. Mr. Stallone modestly told Martin Kasindorf, "I am at the beginning of a new style of actors," though the real precursor of this style was probably Steve Reeves.

CAMPAIGN SLOGAN: "Vote for the Italian Stallion"

PLATFORM: Mr. Stallone promises that *Rambo* will replace Rimbaud in college curricula.
Mr. Stallone promises to arm-wrestle Gorbachev for Europe, winner take all.

RUNNING MATE: Arnold Schwarzenegger*

SHADOW CABINET: Secretary of Defense: Don Knotts**

PITFALL: Hey, wait a doggone minute here. One generation produces Chaplin, the next produces Orson Welles, and ours produces *Stallone?* One is tempted to ask what went haywire? If the voters were to think, Mr. Stallone would bomb at the ballot box. Of course, thoughtful voters would be something of a novelty.

*Mr. Schwarzenegger brings some of the liberal chic of Camelot to the ticket.

**Mr. Knotts offers the Russkies a less menacing image than Mr. Stallone, who is himself less warlike than Caspar Weinberger.

Howard Stern

EXPERIENCE: Mr. Stern hosts a radio program broadcast by Infinity Broadcasting on WXRK-FM in New York and WYSP-FM in Philadelphia during the 6:00 to 10:00 A.M. drive slot. Arbitron says its New York rating is number one, but to the FCC it smells like number two because of Mr. Stern's frank talk and smutty jokes about ess-ee-ex.

WINNABILITY: If Mr. Stern gets the votes of people who like dirty jokes, he is a shoo-in. Most voters like to joke about ess-ee-ex.

CAMPAIGN SLOGAN: "There's No Entendre Like a Double Entendre!"

PLATFORM: Mr. Stern promises to wash the mouths of the FCC prudes because they are obviously obsessed by naughty thoughts. Mr. Stern promises to tell the Ayatollah what he can do with all those missiles he got from Ronald Reagan.

RUNNING MATE: George Carlin*

SHADOW CABINET: Chief of Protocol: Robin Leach
Secretary of State: Erica Jong
Attorney General: Paul Newman**
Press Secretary: Richard Nixon***
Éminence grise: Don Imus

---

*It was the broadcast of a Carlin monologue over Pacifica's WBAI that led to the 1978 Supreme Court case that ruled seven words too naughty for radio. As Mr. Carlin observed, if only seven of the 400,000 words of English are naughty, they must be *very* naughty.

**Mr. Newman says he never knew how to cuss until he starred in *Slap Shot,* possibly the best sports movie ever made because it does not, like so many others, drown in its own schmaltz.

***Mr. Nixon can again use all those expletives deleted from his White House tapes. Seymour Hersch says Nixon cussed so much because he hoped it would make him seem more like a regular guy. Well, it didn't.

PITFALL: During Prohibition, Will Rogers said, "If you think this country ain't Dry, you just watch 'em vote, and if you think this country ain't Wet, you just watch 'em drink." Mr. Stern may encounter the Hypocrisy Factor. Tough #&¢%, Howie!

Meryl Streep

EXPERIENCE: Ms. Streep is widely considered the finest actress now performing in English. She is convincing across a wider range than anyone else.

WINNABILITY: Having attended Vassar and Yale, Ms. Streep is a bit upscale for the average voter, though her Karen Silkwood ought to establish her blue-collar credentials.

CAMPAIGN SLOGAN: "I Can Be Anybody You Want Me to Be"

PLATFORM: Ms. Streep promises to keep American troops out of Africa.

Ms. Streep promises to write her own speeches, as she wrote her own lines for the custody scene in *Kramer vs. Kramer*.
Ms. Streep will establish high standards for safety at nuclear plants.

RUNNING MATE: Oscar

SHADOW CABINET: Everyone who is anyone in Hollywood is eager to work with Ms. Streep. Her cabinet will be star-studded.

PITFALL: Ms. Streep's Karen Silkwood was a flasher. Americans have always expected a male President to be able to keep his shirt on, and they are likely to expect the same from the first woman in the White House.

Dr. Hunter S. Thompson

EXPERIENCE: Dr. Thompson, the mad-dog prince of gonzo journalism, is the model for *Doonesbury*'s Raoul Duke and the Bill Murray character in *Where the Buffalo Roam*.

WINNABILITY: Dr. Thompson's *Fear and Loathing* books about the 1972 campaign are the funniest and among the most insightful about Presidential politics. He lost his Freak Power bid to become sheriff of Aspen but carried three of the six major precincts. He awarded himself the doctorate, so maybe he can award himself the White House.

CAMPAIGN SLOGAN: "Be Angry at the Sun"

PLATFORM: Dr. Thompson promises not to make the kinds of tacky deals that characterize Presidential politics. He says, "Liberalism itself has failed, and for a pretty good reason. It has been too often compromised by the people who represented it."
Dr. Thompson promises to reorganize the Drug Enforcement Agency.

RUNNING MATE: Tom Wolfe

SHADOW CABINET: Press Secretary: I. F. Stone
White House Chef: Calvin Trillin
Campaign Biographer: Terry Southern
Campaign Manager: Gary Hart

PITFALL: Dr. Thompson can be neither outrageous enough to please his fans nor respectable enough to please the mainstream voter. Times are always tough for an aging enfant terrible. If he acts crazy, they scold him for refusing to grow up, and if he doesn't act crazy they say he sold out or lost his magic.

Lily Tomlin

EXPERIENCE: Ms. Tomlin was called "one of the funniest women in the world" by *The New Yorker*. Many people would eliminate "one of" from that observation.

WINNABILITY: As this book goes to press, a discredited hack like George Bush and a nonentity like Skip Gephardt are spoken of as serious candidates (and, heaven help us, they may *be* serious candidates). Ms. Tomlin has been a beloved American institution since she first appeared on *Laugh-In* in 1970, and she can certainly sock it to opponents like these, giving them all the Flying Fickle Finger of Fate Award.

CAMPAIGN SLOGAN: "One ringy-dingy! *Two* ringy-dingies!"

PLATFORM: Ms. Tomlin promises to continue her search for signs of intelligent life in the universe despite the depressing lack of evidence that any will be found on the planet Earth.
Ms. Tomlin promises to work from nine to five without naps.

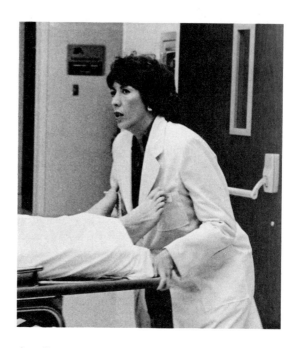

RUNNING MATE: Art Carney

SHADOW CABINET: Chief of Protocol: Mrs. Earbore the Tasteful Lady
Secretary of Labor: Ernestine
Secretary of Education: Suzy Sorority
Press Secretary: Edith Ann
Secretary of Defense: Tommy Velour

PITFALL: Ms. Tomlin plays so many characters so convincingly that voters might worry about which one would be in charge during a crisis.

Desmond Mpico Tutu

EXPERIENCE: Mr. Tutu is Anglican archbishop of Johannesburg. Although he is one of the most famous people in the world, the media always introduce him as "Nobel Peace Prize–Winning Archbishop Desmond Tutu," as if his first name were "Nobel Peace Prize–Winning Archbishop" and his middle name were "Desmond." Well, his middle name is Mpico, the word for *life* in the Bantu language of Sotho.

WINNABILITY: The United States is a curious country. Americans are all for labor unions in Poland and civil rights in South Africa even as unions and civil rights fall on evil days here at home. As a foreigner with a strange accent, Mr. Tutu might prove more acceptable to middle-of-the-road Americans than home-grown activists.

CAMPAIGN SLOGAN: "Boycott Both the Botha Boys"

PLATFORM: Mr. Tutu promises peaceful progress toward racial equality.

RUNNING MATE: Nelson Mandela

SHADOW CABINET: Press Secretaries: Ladysmith Black Mambazo
White House Chaplain: Trevor Huddleston

PITFALL: Mr. Tutu has a funny name. When John Lindsay wore a tutu for a charity fund-raiser, the picture killed his Presidential aspirations. If voters balk at a candidate who wore a tutu, they will certainly balk at a President who is one.

Peter Ueberroth

EXPERIENCE: Mr. Ueberroth ran the 1984 Summer Olympic Games in Los Angeles with a $215 million surplus even though the Russkies refused to play. He is now the avatar of Kenesaw Mountain Landis as commissioner of baseball.

WINNABILITY: Mr. Ueberroth looks and acts like a robot programmed to represent the perfect Republican Presidential candidate as seen in the dreams of the Daughters of the American Revolution. He is both too good to be true and too goody-goody to be believed. This combination might be insufferable at a party but it might also win a Presidential election.

CAMPAIGN SLOGAN: "If He Can Make the MVP Pee in a Jar, He Can Run This Country"

PLATFORM: Mr. Ueberroth will make the government a paying proposition by renting advertising space on the clothing of all civil servants and elected officials.
Mr. Ueberroth will win the War on Drugs by having the National Guard spend its summers uprooting marijuana instead of pretending to kill Russians.

RUNNING MATE: Joseph Jefferson Jackson*

SHADOW CABINET: Secretary of Defense: George Steinbrenner
Secretary of Education: Simone LeVant
Surgeon General: Pippi Longstocking

PITFALL: Voters who tolerated Mr. Ueberroth's blatant commercialization of the Olympics may have done so because the Olympics had long since become tawdry and materialistic. Americans may be less willing to entrust the Constitution to someone who might use it for brand-name endorsements.

*Joseph Jefferson "Shoeless Joe" Jackson was one of the athletes who conspired to fix the 1919 World Series in the Black Sox Scandal, thereby creating the need to have a commissioner of baseball.

Dr. Ruth Westheimer

EXPERIENCE: Dr. Ruth tells Americans how to do things that a generation ago Dr. Kinsey caught hell for hinting that Americans might fantasize about.

WINNABILITY: Most Americans, if you press them off the record, will admit they know little and care less about the international balance of payments or the strategic significance of Chad, but *everybody* cares about the stuff Dr. Ruth explains.

CAMPAIGN SLOGAN: "Learn the Truth from Dr. Ruth"

PLATFORM: Dr. Ruth promises multiple orgasms for voters who mix their tickets.
Dr. Ruth promises executive clemency for Jean Harris.
Dr. Ruth will star in condom ads for ABC, CBS, NBC, PBS, NPR, and ESPN.

RUNNING MATE: Dr. Joyce Brothers

SHADOW CABINET: Surgeon General: The Michelin Man
Secretary of State: Warren Beatty

PITFALL: Dr. Ruth may not be able to use the airwaves now that the FCC has decided to ban risqué palaver.

Vanna White

EXPERIENCE: Ms. White was selected by Merv Griffin from 200 applicants to turn the letters on *Wheel of Fortune*.

WINNABILITY: For turning those letters so skillfully, and for clapping her hands enthusiastically when contestants win something, Ms. White is seen by 43 million Americans every week, a thousand of whom take the time to write her fan letters. Most candidates don't get a thousand fan letters in a lifetime, let alone a week.

CAMPAIGN SLOGAN: "Around and Around and Around I Go, and Where I Stop, Nobody Knows"

PLATFORM: Ms. White promises that Pat Sajak will show his belly button at her inaugural ball, as the madcap host did one day on *W of F.*

Ms. White promises that she will fall on her face in the Oval Office as gracefully as she fell on her face descending the stairs of the puzzle platform the day the guy won the car—every President has to know how to fall on his or her face.

Ms. White told *People* she did not remember the title of the last book she read and she has no lines to learn for *W of F,* but she promises she can read the TelePrompTer as well as The Great Communicator.

RUNNING MATE: Vanessa Williams

SHADOW CABINET: Press Secretary: Frankie Laine

PITFALL: Now that *Playboy* has exposed hitherto secret aspects of her talent, voters may suspect she could be a security risk.

Bruce Willis

EXPERIENCE: Mr. Willis is an experienced Moonlighter who has become hot on TV for the kind of double entendre that has gotten Howard Stern in trouble on radio (e.g., being obsessed with "getting horizontal" with Maddie).

WINNABILITY: Mr. Willis represents the "new machismo," which is like the old machismo but less blatantly sexist. The last of 3,000 actors to read for the part on *Moonlighting,* Mr. Willis skyrocketed to fame. A guy who can fob himself off as a rock star and sell more records than the real rock stars may be able to fob himself off as a politician and get more votes than the real ones.

CAMPAIGN SLOGAN: "A Vote for Bruce Is a Vote for Bruno"

PLATFORM: Mr. Willis promises to promote Seagram's without promoting alcohol abuse.

Mr. Willis promises to combine the urbane appeal of Cary Grant with the inane appeal of the Three Stooges.

RUNNING MATE: David Addison

SHADOW CABINET: First Lady: Kim Basinger

PITFALL: The staying power of Mr. Willis has not been tested. Have you heard much from Henry Winkler lately?

Oprah Winfrey

EXPERIENCE: Ms. Winfrey gets paid to talk to people. This is nice work if you can get it.

WINNABILITY: Ms. Winfrey beat Phil Donahue at the ratings game so she ought to be able to handle this year's crop of candidates.

CAMPAIGN SLOGAN: "Bring Home a Big One to Mama!"

PLATFORM: Ms. Winfrey promises executive clemency for Bigger Thomas.
Ms. Winfrey promises that nudists will be invited to her inaugural ball.
Ms. Winfrey promises to ad-lib her State of the Union messages because her scripted interview with Tom Selleck was a dud compared to the ones she wings.

RUNNING MATE: Whoopi Goldberg

SHADOW CABINET: Secretary of State: Stephen Spielberg
Press Secretary: Johnny Carson

PITFALL: Ms. Winfrey first gained prominence as Miss Tennessee. Given the dubious track record of former beauty queens like Bess Myerson and Vanessa Williams, voters may prefer women candidates who seem less dangerously glamorous.

Ken Lawless

EXPERIENCE: Mr. Lawless is the perpetrator of this opus.

WINNABILITY: As the candidate least likely to garner a single vote, Mr. Lawless is the freest to speak his mind.

CAMPAIGN SLOGAN: "Power Tends to Corrupt and Satire Tends to Close Saturday Night"

PLATFORM: Mr. Lawless promises to resign as soon as he is inaugurated in favor of his Vice President, a man of wit, wisdom, compassion, and commitment.

RUNNING MATE: Kurt Vonnegut, Jr.

SHADOW CABINET: Secretary of Defense: Sheriff Destry
Secretary of Commerce: Phineas Taylor Barnum
Secretary of State: Ben Turpin
Secretary of Education: Mae West
Press Secretary: Judy Tenuta
Ambassador to the United Nations: Tina Turner
Chairman of the Federal Communications Commission: Benny Hill

PITFALL: As a candidate for the highest office in the land, Mr. Lawless might be tempted to take himself seriously. So many candidates *do,* you know.